Please renew or return items by the date shown on your receipt

www.hertsdirect.org/libraries

Renewals and enquiries: 0300 123 4049

Textphone for hearing or speech impaired: 0300 123 4041

STE

Credits

Footprint credits
Editor: Jo Williams
Production and layout: Emma Bryers
Maps: Kevin Feeney

Managing Director: Andy Riddle
Commercial Director: Patrick Dawson
Publisher: Alan Murphy
Publishing Managers: Felicity Laughton,
Jo Williams, Nicola Gibbs
Marketing and Partnerships Director:
Liz Harper
Marketing Executive: Liz Eyles
Trade Product Manager: Diane McEntee
Account Managers: Paul Bew, Tania Ross
Advertising: Renu Sibal, Elizabeth Taylor
Trade Product Co-ordinator: Kirsty Holmes

Photography credits
Front cover: Dreamstime
Back cover: Shutterstock

Printed in Great Britain by CPI Antony Rowe,
Chippenham, Wiltshire

Publishing information
Footprint *Focus Kuala Lumpur &*
Malaysian Peninsula
1st edition
© Footprint Handbooks Ltd
September 2012

ISBN: 978 1 908206 79 4
CIP DATA: A catalogue record for this book
is available from the British Library

® Footprint Handbooks and the Footprint
mark are a registered trademark of
Footprint Handbooks Ltd

Published by Footprint
6 Riverside Court
Lower Bristol Road
Bath BA2 3DZ, UK
T +44 (0)1225 469141
F +44 (0)1225 469461
footprinttravelguides.com

Distributed in the USA by Globe Pequot
Press, Guilford, Connecticut

The content of Footprint *Focus Kuala
Lumpur & Malaysian Peninsula* has been
taken directly from Footprint's *Southeast
Asia Handbook* which was researched and
written by Andrew Spooner and Paul Dixon.

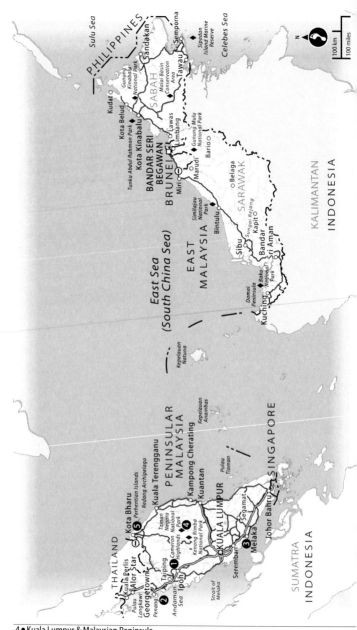

Malaya is a word infused with the mystery of the East. It conjures up images of sultans and headhunters; munificent jungles brimming with exotic wildlife and the clippers of Conrad's era cutting through the warm waters of the South China Sea. Of course Malaya became Malaysia and embraced modernity: the jungles are contained in national parks or have been ploughed up into rubber and palm oil plantations; the relatively new city of Kuala Lumpur is a modern metropolis of glass; and container ships, not clippers, now plough up and down the Strait of Melaka.

Even so, Malaysia retains its cross-cultural stamp with the sharp spices of its Indian markets, its red Buddhist temples and the prayer call of the muezzin echoing from mosques. Sandwiched between Singapore to the south, the island of Sumatra to the west and Thailand to the north, the Peninsula states support the great bulk of the country's population. And, just as Malaysia itself is a country of two halves, so the Peninsula too can be divided into a vibrant western side and a bucolic east separated by the Barisan Titiwangsa, the Peninsula's jungled spine. Malaysian Borneo – the states of Sabah and Sarawak – dovetails more closely with the romantic vision of 'Malaya'. The countryside remains dominated by tribal groups, collectively known as Dayaks, and much of it is still forested.

Contemporary Malaysia is a land forging ahead towards a vision of full development, with its car factories, glam KL vodka bars and big-name global events such as the annual Formula1 race. The country's rich multi-cultural heritage is to be found everywhere, with pensioners describing an education with strict Irish brothers; graveyards littered with the bones of the early colonists, and later with troops cut down in the Second World War; and tales of huge Chinese galleons laden with gold and silk. This exotic fusion of cultures is shown nightly on the nation's dinner plates with Nyonya, Indian, Chinese and Eurasian cuisine offering visitors a tantalizing insight into the sophistication of a typical Malaysian's tastebuds and into the heady history of this sultry and enticing land.

Planning your trip

Getting to Kuala Lumpur and Malaysian Peninsula

Air
The majority of visitors arrive at **Kuala Lumpur International Airport** (**KLIA**). Some international flights go direct to Langkawi and Penang. ➤➤ *For airport tax, see page 16.*

From Southeast Asia There are flights to Kuala Lumpur (KL) from all regional capitals. AirAsia (www.airasia.com) has flights connecting KL with Jakarta, Denpasar, Yogyakarta, Medan, Padang, Makassar, Bandung, Singapore, Hanoi, Ho Chi Minh City, Phnom Penh Siem Reap, Vientiane, Yangon and Bangkok. AirAsia also connects Bangkok with Penang and Johor Bahru. Many airlines fly from Hong Kong, Manila and Tokyo. Budget carriers now fly between KL and Singapore, including **Tiger Airways** (www.tigerairways.com) **Jetstar Asia** (www.jetstar.com) and **AirAsia**. Malaysia Airlines subsidiary **Firefly** (www.fireflyz.com.my) offers flights to cities in Malaysia, Indonesia, Singapore and Thailand from its base in Subang, KL.

Note that budget airlines arrive and depart from KLIA **LCCT** (Low Cost Carrier Terminal) some 20 minutes' drive from the main KLIA terminal building. All other flights depart from **Subang Airport**, closer to KL city centre.

Boat
From **Sumatra**, ferries run regularly from Dumai to Melaka. Passenger boats connect Langkawi Island with Satun in southern **Thailand**. Small boats run between **Singapore**'s Changi Point and Johor state.

Rail
Keretapi Tanah Melayu (**KTM**), www.ktmb.com.my, runs express trains daily between Singapore and the major cities on the west coast of Malaysia. There is a daily express train from Bangkok to Butterworth. This connects with the KL service, and from KL onwards to Singapore.

The most luxurious way to travel by train to Malaysia is aboard the **Eastern & Oriental Express** (E&O).

Road
It is possible to travel to Malaysia overland by bus or shared taxi from Thailand and Singapore. Direct buses and taxis are much easier than the local alternatives, which terminate at the borders. **Singapore** is six hours by taxi from KL (via Johor Bahru) and about seven hours by bus. Taxi fares are approximately double bus fares.

There are direct buses and taxis from **Thailand** to most major towns in northern Malaysia and six border crossing points. For those using the north–south highway – which is most people – the crossing point is at Bukit Kayu Hitam, which links up with the Thai city of Hat Yai. On the western side of the Peninsula there are also crossings at Wang Kelian and Padang Besar. The Wang Kelian crossing to Satun in Thailand, is convenient if you are driving; it is quiet and usually pretty quick. The Padang Besar crossing is easy on foot and makes sense if travelling to Pulau Langkawi. In Perak the crossing is at Pengkalan Hulu

Don't miss…

Numbers relate to map on page 4.

and in Kelantan, on the eastern side of the Peninsula there are two more crossing points: Pengkalan Kubar, and from Kota Bahru to Rantau Panjang/Sungai Golok. The more popular of these is the Rantau Panjang crossing; few people cross at Pengkalan Kubar. **Note** The southern Thai provinces suffer from serious separatist violence. Bombings and shootings occur daily, with fatalities. Check the situation if you intend to cross the border. At present, a state of emergency exists in the southern Thai provinces of Pattani, Narathiwat, Songkhla and Yala and the UK Foreign Office recommends against all but the most essential travel to the Thai border provinces (check www.fco.gov.uk for details). Local buses and taxis terminate at the border crossings, but there are regular onward connections on each side.

Transport in Kuala Lumpur and Malaysian Peninsula

Air
In a bid to counter the aggressive marketing of **AirAsia**, **MAS** offer excellent 'what you see is what you pay' fares, with all-inclusive domestic airfares starting at 69RM. These fares are offered sporadically and can be found online or in local media.

Another MAS subsidiary, **Firefly** (www.fireflyz.com.my) offers good coverage of Peninsula Malaysia, and has some destinations in Indonesia and Thailand. Firefly uses the airport at Subang for connections on the peninsula and Thailand, Singapore and Indonesia.

The budget airline **AirAsia**, www.airasia.com, flies to Alor Star, Bintulu, Johor Bahru (JB), KL, Kuala Terengganu, Kota Baru, Langkawi and Penang. Domestic flights from KL leave from the LCCT (Low Cost Carrier Terminal) 20 km from KLIA, see page 19. **▸▸** *For airport tax, see page 16.*

Boat
There are regular scheduled ferry services between the main islands – Pangkor, Penang and Langkawi – and the mainland. There are passenger and car ferries between Butterworth and Georgetown (Penang), every 20 minutes. For other offshore islands, mostly off the east coast, fishing boats, and sometimes regular boats, leave from the nearest fishing port. Pulau Tioman is accessed from Mersing. There is still some river transport on the Peninsula's east coast.

Rail
The **KTM** train (see Rail, page 6) is an economical and comfortable way to travel around the Peninsula. However, trains are much slower than buses and often arrive at awkward times in the middle of the night.

There are two main lines. One runs up the west coast from Singapore, through KL, Ipoh and Butterworth, connecting with Thai railways at Padang Besar. The other line branches off from the west coast line at Gemas (halfway between KL and Singapore) and heads northeast to Kota Bahru. The express service (*Ekspres Rakyat* or *Ekspres Sinaran*) only stops at major towns; the regular service stops at every station but is slightly cheaper. All overnight trains have sleeping berths and all classes have air conditioning (very cold). Reservations can be made for both classes. First- and second-class carriages are equipped with videos.

Road

Bus Peninsula Malaysia has an excellent bus system with a network of public express buses and several privately run services. Air-conditioned express buses connect the major towns; seats can be reserved and prices are reasonable. The air conditioning is often very cold. Prices vary between companies. Note that buses are less frequent on the east coast.

Recommended companies are **Plusliner**, T03-2274 0499, www.plusliner.com, and **Transnasional**, T03-4047 7878, www.transnasional.com.my. Although these may cost a few ringgit more, it's usually money well spent. In larger towns there may be a number of bus stops. Increasingly, long-distance bus terminals are being built outside of major towns, often necessitating a taxi ride into town.

Car and motorbike Car hire companies are listed in the transport listings of individual towns. Visitors can hire a car provided they are have an international driving licence, are aged 23-65 and have had a licence for at least a year. Car hire costs RM100-250 per day. Cheaper weekly and monthly rates and special deals are available.

Driving is on the left; give way to drivers on the right. However, local drivers often don't obey traffic lights or road signs and hardly ever give way so you will need to have your wits about you. Within towns the speed limit is 50 kph; the wearing of seat belts is compulsory for front seat passengers and the driver. Most roads are kept in good repair. However, during the monsoon season, heavy rains may make some east coast travel difficult and the west coast roads can be congested.

Cycling Bicycles are available for hire from some guesthouses and hire shops, especially on islands such as Pangkor, Penang, Langkawi and Tioman, but also in some towns and hill resorts. Compared with motorbikes, bike hire can seem expensive – RM10-20 per day and substantially more by the hour. Prices vary a good deal depending on the type of bike.

Touring, hybrid or mountain bikes are fine for most roads and tracks in Malaysia. Mountain bikes have made a big impact in the country, so accessories and spares are widely available. Less common are components made of unusual materials, such as titanium and composites. Cycling clubs are springing up across the country. Unlike Indonesia and Thailand, a foreigner on a bike is not such an object of interest. Cars and buses rarely give way to a bicycle so be very wary; avoid major roads and major towns. Cheaper buses usually carry bicycles, but air-conditioned tour buses may refuse. Many international airlines transport bicycles for no extra cost, provided they are not boxed. Take the pedals off and deflate the tyres.

Useful items include: pollution mask if travelling to large cities; puncture repair kit; spare inner tubes; spare tyre; pump; a good map; bungee cords; and a water filter.

Taxi There are two types of taxi in Malaysia: local and 'out-station' (long-distance). The latter, usually Mercedes or Peugeot, connect all major towns and cities. They operate on a shared-cost basis; as soon as there are four passengers, the taxis set off. It is possible to

arter the whole taxi for the price of four single fares. Taxi stands are usually next door to
ajor bus stations. If shared, taxi fares usually cost about twice as much as bus fares, but
ey are much faster. For groups travelling together taking a taxi makes good sense. It is
asier to find other passengers in the morning than later in the day.

Local taxi fares in Malaysia are fairly cheap, but it is rare to find a taxi with a meter
xcept in KL); you will need to bargain. On the east coast, air-conditioned taxis cost more.

ishaws In KL it has long been too dangerous for trishaws, apart from around Chinatown
nd suburban areas. In towns such as Melaka, Georgetown and Kota Bharu, as well as in
any other smaller towns, trishaws are still available but they have largely become an
xpensive way to travel for well-heeled tourists. Bargaining over fares is acceptable.

laps

aps are widely available in Malaysia. Road maps are on sale at most petrol stations;
etronas produces an excellent atlas, *Touring Malaysia by Road*. Good country maps include
elles *Malaysia* (1:1,500,000) and *West Malaysia* (1:650,000). The Malaysian tourist board
roduces a good map of Kuala Lumpur and a series of state maps, although these are much
oorer in quality.

Where to stay in Kuala Lumpur and Malaysian Peninsula

alaysia offers a good selection of international-standard hotels as well as simpler hotels,
id-range business hotels and has some of Southeast Asia's best guesthouses and hostels
r those travelling on a budget. Room rates are subject to 5-10% tax. Many of the major
ternational chains have hotels, such as **Hilton**, **Holiday Inn** and **Hyatt**. Room rates in the
ig hotels have been fairly stable for the last few years. The number of four- and five-star
otel rooms has also multiplied. This has forced hotels to keep prices highly competitive.
y world standards even the most expensive hotels are good value.

It is also worth noting that in tourist resorts, many hotels have two, sometimes three,
oom tariffs: one for weekdays, one for weekends and sometimes a third for holiday
eriods. Room rates can vary substantially between these periods. In the more popular
oliday destinations like the Cameron Highlands, accommodation can become scarce
uring the school holidays (March, May-June, August and mid-November to early January)
nd prices sky rocket. During these months it is worth booking ahead.

On the east coast of Peninsula Malaysia it is often possible to stay with families in Malay
ampongs (villages) as part of the homestay programme (contact the local tourist office
r travel agent for more information). The most popular place to do this is at Kampong
herating, north of Kuantan, although it has been getting progressively quieter in recent
ears as backpackers hunt out newer pastures; it is also possible to stay in a kampong
ouse in Merang.

Towns and cities on the tourist trail also often have guesthouses with dorms for the
eriously shallow of pocket. These vary in quality, but most major tourist centres have a
ood selection to choose from and there are some superb dorms in Malaysia.

Reflecting Malaysia's enthusiastic embrace of all things high-tech, most hotels, and
ven many guesthouses, have internet access. Wi-Fi is becoming a standard offering in
ourist centres.

Price codes

Where to stay

$$$$ over US$100 $$$ US$46-100

$$ US$20-45 $ under US$20

Prices include taxes and service charge, but not meals. They are based on a double room, except in the $ range, where prices are almost always per person.

Restaurants

$$$ over US$12 $$ US$6-12 $ under US$6

Prices refer to the cost of a two-course meal, not including drinks.

Food and drink in Kuala Lumpur and Malaysian Peninsula

Cuisine

Malaysians love their food, and the dishes of the three main communities – Malay, Chinese and Indian – comprise a hugely varied national menu. Every state has its own **Malay** dishes. The staple diet is rice and curry, which is rich and creamy due to the use of coconut milk. Herbs and spices include chillis, tamarind, ginger, turmeric, coriander, lemongrass, anise, cloves, cumin, caraway and cinnamon. Favourite dishes include satay, *nasi campur* (rice with a selection of meat, fish, vegetables and fruit), *nasi goreng* (rice with meat and vegetables fried with garlic, onions and sambal) and *nasi lemak* (a breakfast dish of rice cooked in coconut milk and served with prawn *sambal*, *ikan bilis* – whole deep fried anchovy – a hard boiled egg, peanuts and cucumber).

The former Straits Settlements of Penang and Melaka have an amalgamation of Chinese and Malay cuisine called **Nyonya** (also known as Straits Chinese). Nyonya food is spicier than Chinese food and, unlike Malay cuisine, uses pork. In Penang the dishes have adopted flavours from neighbouring Thailand, whereas Melaka's Nyonya food has Indonesian overtones. Emphasis is placed on presentation and the fine-chopping of ingredients.

Cantonese and Hainanese cooking are the most prevalent **Chinese** cuisines in Malaysia. Some of the more common dishes are Hainanese chicken rice (rice cooked in chicken stock and served with steamed or roast chicken), *char kway teow* (Teochew-style fried noodles with eggs, cockles and chilli paste), *luak* (Hokkien oyster omelette), *dim sum* (steamed dumplings and patties), *yong tau foo* (beancurd and vegetables stuffed with fish) and *bak kut teh* (pork rib herbal soup). Steamboat, the Chinese answer to fondue, consists of thinly sliced pieces of raw meat, fish, prawns, cuttlefish, fishballs and vegetables tossed into a bubbling cauldron of stock in the centre of the table. They are then dunked into hot chilli and soy sauces and the resulting soup provides a flavoursome broth to wash it all down. Often a lot of MSG is added to the stock resulting in a parched thirst after dining. Try and find a place that doesn't use MSG and you'll be well rewarded.

Many of the more religiously inclined ethnic Chinese are strong adherents to vegetarianism and in towns with a major Chinese population, it is usually easy to find a decent Chinese pure vegetarian eatery complete with authentic pieces of mock meat made from soya.

With a large ethnic **Indian** population, vegetarian food is usually available. North Indian dishes tend to be subtly spiced, use more meat (no beef) and are served with bread. Southern dishes use fiery spices, emphasize vegetables and are served with rice. Pancake nclude *roti*, *dosai* and *chapati*. Malaysia's famous *mamak*-men are Indian Muslims who are highly skilled in everything from *teh tarik* (see Drink, below) to rotis.

Eating out

Malaysia has everything from street stalls to swanky international restaurants. The cheapest, and often the best, places to eat are in **hawker centres** and roadside stalls (usually close to night markets), where you can eat well for RM3-4. Stalls generally serve Malay, Indian or Chinese dishes. **Kedai kopi** (coffee shops) can be found on almost every street; a meal costs from RM5. Usually run by Chinese or Indian families, they open at around 0900 and close in the early evening, many are 24 hours. Some open at dawn to serve dim sum to commuters on the way to work.

Restaurants geared to travellers tend to be concentrated in beach resorts and serve staples such as banana pancakes, pseudo-pizza and pasta dishes, smoothies and toasted sandwiches.

Drink

Soft drinks, mineral water and freshly squeezed fruit juices are readily available. **Anchor** and **Tiger** beer are widely sold, except in the more strict Islamic states of the east coast such as Kelantan, and are cheapest at the hawker stalls (RM5-7 per bottle). A beer costs RM8-15 per bottle in coffee shops. Potent Malaysian-brewed **Guinness Foreign Extra** is popular; the Chinese believe it has medicinal qualities. Malaysian tea is grown in the Cameron Highlands and is very good. One of the most interesting cultural refinements of the Indian Muslim community is the *mamak*-man, who is famed for *teh tarik* (pulled tea), which is thrown dramatically from one cup to another with no spillages. The idea is to cool it down, but it has become an art form. Most coffee comes from Indonesia, although some is locally produced. Malaysians like strong coffee and unless you specify *kurang manis* (less sugar), *tak mahu manis* (no sugar) or *kopi kosong* (black, no sugar), it will come with lashings of condensed milk. To ask for tea or coffee without sugar or milk ask for teh (tea)/*kopi* (coffee) *o kosong*.

Festivals in Kuala Lumpur and Malaysian Peninsula

The timing of Islamic festivals is calculated on the basis of local sightings of various phases of the moon. Dates are approximations and can vary by a day or two. Muslim festivals move forward by around nine or 10 days each year. Chinese, Indian (Hindu) and some Christian holidays are also movable. Sultans' and governors' birthday celebrations are marked with processions and festivities. State holidays can disrupt travel, particularly in east coast states where they run for several days. Each state also has its own public holidays when shops and banks close. Schools in Malaysia have four breaks throughout the year. Dates vary from state to state but generally fall in the months of March (one week), May to June (two weeks), August (one week) and November to January (six weeks). To check dates for all festivals visit www.tourism.gov.my. Popular festivals include:

Jan-Feb Thaipusam, celebrated by Hindus during the full moon. Devotees pay homage to Lord Muraga by piercing their bodies, cheeks and tongues with *vel* (skewers) and hooks weighted with oranges, and carrying *kevadis* (steel structures bearing the image of the Lord). Thousands of pilgrims gather at Batu Caves near KL (see page 26).
Jan-Feb Chinese New Year, a 15-day lunar festival that sees Chinatown streets crowded with shoppers buying oranges to signify luck. Lion, unicorn or dragon dances welcome in

the New Year and thousands of firecrackers are ignited to ward off evil spirits.

Jun The Dragon Boat Festival honours the ancient Chinese poet hero, Qu Yuan who drowned himself in a protest against corruption. His death is commemorated with dragon boat races and the eating of dumplings; the biggest celebrations are in Penang.

Aug Mooncake or Lantern Festival. Marking the overthrow of the Mongol Dynasty in China, this is celebrated with the eating of mooncakes and the lighting of festive lanterns.

Aug Festival of the Hungry Ghosts. Souls in purgatory return to earth to feast. Food is offered to the spirits. Altars are set up in the streets and candles with faces are burned.

Aug–Sep Awal Ramadan, the first day of Ramadan. Muslims must abstain from all food and drink (as well as smoking) from sunrise to sundown. Every evening stalls sell traditional Malay cakes and delicacies.

Oct Festival of the Nine Emperor Gods. This marks the return of the emperor god spirits to earth. Mediums go into a trance and are carried on chairs comprised of sharp blades or spikes. A strip of yellow cotton is worn on the right wrist as a sign of devotion. Ceremonies may end with a firewalking ritual.

Oct-Nov Deepavali, the Hindu festival of lights commemorates the victory of good over evil and the triumphant return of Rama. Hindu homes are brightly decorated for the occasion.

Local customs and laws in Kuala Lumpur and Malaysian Peninsula

Conduct As elsewhere in Southeast Asia, 'losing face' brings shame. Using a loud voice or wild gesticulations will be taken to signify anger and, hence, 'loss of face'. Similarly, the person you shout at will also feel loss of face, especially in public. In Muslim company it is impolite to touch others with the left hand. Men shake hands but men don't usually shake a woman's hand, except in Kuala Lumpur. Using the index finger to point is insulting; the thumb or whole hand should be used to wave down a taxi. Before entering a private home, remove your shoes; it is usual to take a small gift for the host, not opened until after the visitor has left.

Dress Malaysians dress for the heat. Clothes are light, cool and casual but tidy, especially in cities; tourists in shorts and flip-flops may look out of place in KL, but are an accepted part of the city's modern culturescape. Exclusive restaurants may require formal wear. Although many Malaysian business people have adopted the Western jacket and tie, the batik shirt, or *baju*, is the traditional formal wear for men; women wear the graceful *sarung kebaya*.

Dress codes are important to observe from the point of view of Islamic sensitivities particularly on the Peninsula's east coast. Topless sunbathing is completely taboo, and in some places (such as Marang or Kelantan) bikinis will cause great offence. In Muslim areas women should keep shoulders covered and wear below-knee skirts or trousers. A wedding ring may help ward off the attentions of amorous admirers. Malaysia's cross-cultural differences are most apparent on the streets: many Chinese girls think nothing of wearing brief mini-skirts and shorts, while their Malay counterparts are clad from head to toe.

Prohibitions Malaysia is well known around the world for its stringent laws against drugs and there is a mandatory death sentence upon conviction for anyone in possession of 15 g or more of heroin or morphine, 200 g of cannabis or hashish or 40 g of cocaine. Those caught with more than 10 g of heroin or 100 g of cannabis are deemed to be traffickers and face lengthy jail sentences and flogging with a rotan cane.

While alcohol is not illegal in any part of Malaysia, be aware of Muslim sensibilities, particularly in the east coast states of Kelantan and Terengganu.

Religion Remove shoes before entering mosques and Hindu/Buddhist temples. In mosques, women should cover heads, shoulders and legs; men should wear long trousers.

Shopping in Kuala Lumpur and Malaysian Peninsula

Most big towns have modern shopping complexes as well as shops and markets. Department stores are fixed price, but nearly everywhere else it is possible to bargain. At least 30% can be knocked off the price; your first offer should be roughly half the first quote.

What to buy

The islands of Langkawi, Tioman and Labuan have duty-free shopping; the range of goods is poor, however. Electronic, computer and camera equipment are cheaper in Singapore. Kuala Lumpur and most state capitals have a Chinatown, which usually has a few curio shops and a *pasar malam* (night market). Indian quarters, which are invariably labelled 'Little India', are found in bigger towns and are the best places to buy sarongs, *longis*, *dotis* and saris (mostly imported from India) as well as other textiles. Malay handicrafts are usually only found in markets or government craft centres.

Handicrafts

The Malaysian arts and crafts industry has suffered as craftspeople head to the cities in search of more lucrative jobs. The growth of tourism in recent years has helped to reinvigorate it, particularly in traditional handicraft-producing areas, such as the east coast states of Terengganu and Kelantan. The **Malay Arts and Crafts Society** set up Karyaneka centres to market Malaysian arts and crafts in KL and state capitals. Typical handicrafts that can be found on the Peninsula include woodcarvings, batik, *songket* (cloth woven with gold and silver thread), pewterware, silverware, kites, tops and *wayang kulit* (shadow puppets).

Entertainment in Kuala Lumpur and Malaysian Peninsula

Bars and clubs

If you want to stagger down the street five sheets to the wind on a nightly basis, it should be remembered that Malaysia is most certainly not Koh Phangan. There has never been a really happening club scene in Malaysia, although KL has a range of decent clubs and bars, and the nightlife is becoming increasingly sophisticated in the city. Karaoke is a more popular alternative. The main towns where there is a nightlife of sorts are KL and Penang. Despite the lack of booze on the east coast, the Perhentians and Pulau Tioman can get lively after dark if you know the right spots.

Essentials A-Z

Accident and emergency

Ambulance, fire and police, T999. The worldwide emergency number 112 used on GSM phones is redirected to the emergency services in Malaysia.

Customs and duty free

For import, you can bring in 200 cigarettes, 50 cigars or 225g of tobacco and 1 litre of liquor or wine. Cameras, watches, pens, lighters, cosmetics, perfumes and portable music players are duty free. Visitors bringing in dutiable goods such as electronic equipment may have to pay a refundable deposit for temporary importation. It is advisable to carry receipts to avoid this.

Export permits are required for animals and plants, gold, platinum, precious stones and jewellery (except reasonable personal effects) amongst other items. To export antiques a permit must be acquired from Director General of Museums, Muzium Negara, Kuala Lumpur; see page 25.

Electricity

220-240 volts, 50 cycle AC. Some hotels supply adaptors.

Internet

Malaysia is one of the most forward thinking countries in Asia when it comes to information technology and the internet. In line with this, internet cafés have sprung up all over the place. Rates are cheap too: RM2 per hr at the bottom end, with most places charging around RM3 per hr. Generally, internet cafés geared to tourists are more expensive than those serving the local market, where teenage boys spend hours playing online games. For travellers with laptops, guesthouses, hotels, cafés and coffee shops routinely offer free Wi-Fi internet.

Language

The national language is **Bahasa Melayu** (normally shortened to Bahasa). It is very similar to Bahasa Indonesia. All communities, Malay, Chinese and Indian speak Malay. Nearly everyone in Malaysia speaks some English, except in remote areas. Chinese is also spoken, mainly Hokkien but also Cantonese, Hakka, Teochew and Mandarin. The Indian languages of Tamil and Punjabi are spoken too.

Language courses are available in KL (ask at the Tourism Malaysia office, see page 21) and other big cities. A recommended teach-yourself book is *Everyday Malay* by Thomas G Oey (Periplus Language Books, 1995), which is widely available. A Malay/English dictionary or phrase book is also useful.

The basic grammar is very simple, with no tenses, genders or articles. Stress is usually placed on the second syllable of a word. The **a** is pronounced as *ah* in an open syllable, or as in *but* for a closed syllable; **e** is pronounced as in *open* or *bed*; **i** is pronounced as in *feel*; **o** is pronounced as in *all*; **u** is pronounced as in *foot*. The letter **c** is pronounced *ch* as in *change* or *chat*. The **r** is rolled. For useful phrases, see box, opposite.

Media

The main English-language dailies are *The New Straits Times* (www.nst.com.my), *Business Times* (www.btimes.com.my), *The Star* (www.thestar.com.my), which is the best for local news, and *The Malay Mail* (www.mmail.com.my), which is an afternoon paper and basically a gossip rag. The main Sunday papers are *The New Sunday Times*, *The Sunday Mail* and *The Sunday Star*. The English-language dailies are government-owned and this is reflected in their content which tends

Useful words and phrases

Yes/no	Ia/tidak	I'm fine	Baik
Thank you	Terimah kasih	Excuse me/sorry	Ma'af saya
You're welcome	Sama-sama	Where's the...?	Dimana...
Good morning	Selamat pagi	How much is this...?	Ini berapa?
Good afternoon	Selamat petang	My name is...	Nama saya...
How are you?	Apa kabar?	What is your name?	Apa nama anda?

to be relentlessly pro-government. *The Rocket* is the Democratic Action Party's opposition newspaper, and also presents an alternative perspective. International editions of leading foreign newspapers and news magazines can be obtained at main news stands and book stalls, although some are not until mid-afternoon. One of the most popular online news portals is *Malaysia Kini* (www.malaysiakini.com) offering fairly independent coverage of news and politics.

For what's on listings, the best sources are *Time Out KL*, www.timeoutkl.com, and the 'What's On' section of the *Malay Mail*.

There are 6 government **radio** stations in various languages including English. In KL you can tune into the Federal Capital's radio station; there are a number of local stations. The *BBC World Service* can be picked up on FM in southern Johor, from the Singapore transmitter. Elsewhere it can be received on shortwave. The main frequencies are (in kHz): 11750, 9740, 6195 and 3915.

RTM1 and RTM2 are operated by **Radio Television Malaysia**, the government-run station. Some American and British series are shown. Singaporean programmes can be received as far north as Melaka. Satellite and cable TV is widely available. Many hotels carry the ASTRO service, which offers HBO, STAR movies, ESPN, CNN, BBC, Discovery and MTV as well as a host of Chinese channels.

Money

Exchange rates: for up-to-the-minute exchange rates visit www.xe.com.

The unit of currency in Malaysia is the Malaysian dollar or ringgit (RM), which is divided into 100 cents or sen. Bank notes come in denominations of RM1, 5, 10, 50, and 100. Coins are issued in 5, 10, 20 and 50 sen.

Cost of travelling Malaysia is good value. If you stay in the bottom-end guesthouses, eat at hawker centres and use public transport, you can get by on US$20-30 (RM60-90) per day. Cheaper guesthouses charge US$10-15 (RM30-50) a night for 2 people. Dorms are available in big towns, US$3-10 (RM10-30). It is usually possible to find a simple a/c room for US$15-30 (RM40-90). A tourist-class hotel, with a/c, room service, restaurant and swimming pool costs RM100-150. International-class hotels charge RM300-500.

Eating out is also cheap: a good curry can cost as little as US$0.50-1 (RM2-4). Overland travel is a bargain.

A service charge of 10% is automatically added to restaurant and hotel bills, plus a 5% government tax (indicated by the + and ++ signs). For personal services, such as porters, a modest tip is appropriate.

Exchange Cash advances can be issued against credit cards in most banks. Many ATMs wll accept foreign credit and debit cards. Banks with such ATM services include Maybank, HSBC and OCBC TCs can be exchanged at banks and money changers although rates and charges vary.

Opening hours

Most government offices (including some tourist offices and post offices) are closed on the 1st and 3rd Sat of each month. In Terengganu and Kelantan states, weekend days are Thu-Fri, as many Muslim residents visit the mosques for prayers on Fri.

Post

Malaysia's postal service is cheap and reliable, although incoming and outgoing parcels should be registered. Post office opening hours are Mon-Sat 0830-1700. Poste Restante is available at post offices in major cities; make sure your family name is capitalized and underlined. You can also buy AirAsia tickets at post offices.

Safety

Normal precautions should be taken with passports and valuables; many hotels have safes. Pickpocketing and bag snatching are problems in KL, JB and Penang. Women travelling alone need have few worries – although take the usual precautions like not walking alone in deserted places at night.

Tax

Airport departure tax RM15 for domestic flights, RM51 for international, but these are usually included in the ticket price.
GST Sales tax is generally 10%.

Telephone → *Country code +60.*
IDD code 00. Operator T101.
Directory enquiries T102/103.
International operator T108.

TM italk gives excellent rates for international calls, around RM10 for 1 hr. However, you can't call from all public phones in Malaysia; find a phone before you buy a card. Buying a local mobile and Sim card is cheap and easy. Celcom, DiGi and Maxis are the main providers. You can use mobiles with italk cards, but you need to pay local call rates in addition to the italk card itself.

Time

8 hrs ahead of GMT.

Tourist information

The main Tourism Malaysia (www.tourism malaysia.gov.my) office is in KL (see page 21) but it has branches in most large towns. It is very efficient and can help with itineraries, bookings for travel and cultural events and provide information on hotels, restaurants and transport timetables and prices. If there is no Tourism Malaysia office in a town, travel agents are usually helpful.

The Malaysia Tourism Centre is another tourist information bureau (see page 21). Regional tourism offices in state capitals are all reasonably efficient.

For events listings, try *Time Out Kuala Lumpur* (www.timeoutkl.com), and the 'What's On' section of the *Malay Mail*.

Useful websites

www.aseansec.org Government statistics, acronyms and information.
www.malaysiakini.com Excellent and uncensored online Malaysian news portal.
www.journeymalaysia.com Covers the majority of Malaysia's tourist sites in an entertaining and factual way. Books tours.
www.virtualtourist.com A good website with content by other travellers.

Visas and immigration

No visa is required for a stay of up to 3 months in Malaysia (provided you are not going to work) for citizens of the UK, USA, Australia, New Zealand, Canada, Ireland and most other European countries. If you intend to stay longer, 2-month extensions are usually easy to get at immigration offices in KL, Penang or JB. Note that Israeli passport holders are not allowed to enter Malaysia.

Contents

Kuala Lumpur

Kuala Lumpur

In the space of a century, Kuala Lumpur grew from a trading post and tin-mining shanty town into a colonial capital of 1.5 million people. Today it is a modern, cosmopolitan business hub and centre of government. The economic boom that started in the late 1980s has caused a building bonanza to rival that of Singapore. In downtown Kuala Lumpur, old and new are juxtaposed. The jungled backdrop of the Supreme Court's copper-topped clocktower has been replaced by scores of stylish high-rise office blocks, dominated by the soaring, angular-roofed Maybank headquarters. The Victorian, Moorish and Moghul-style buildings, the art deco Central Market, and the Chinese shophouses stand in marked contrast to these impressive skyscrapers. The Petronas Twin Towers offer the most impressive addition to the modern skyline and are part of the Kuala Lumpur City Centre (KLCC) development.

Arriving in Kuala Lumpur

Getting there

Kuala Lumpur (KL) is well linked to the rest of Malaysia and to the wider world. **Kuala Lumpur International Airport (KLIA)** ① *Sepang, 72 km south, T03-8776 2000, www.klia.com.my,* provides a slick point of entry. Glitzy and high-tech, it has all the usual facilities including restaurants, shops and banks. The **Tourism Malaysia** desk has pamphlets and a useful map.

Some domestic air connections (including to Sabah and Sarawak) pass through KLIA, although the **Low Cost Carrier Terminal (LCCT)** ① *20 km south of KLIA, www.lcct.com.my,* is used by most budget airlines. Shuttle buses connect KLIA and the LCCT (20 minutes) for RM1.50. Always check your ticket to confirm which terminal you're flying from.

The LCCT terminal is dominated by the hugely successful **AirAsia** ① *T03-8775 4000, www.airasia.com,* which is the region's main low-cost carrier, with flights as far afield as China, Australia and the UK. Internet bookings provide the best deals. Tickets booked a few weeks in advance are the cheapest and most travellers moving onto Malaysian Borneo find this is the most convenient option. Travel passes are available.

In 2007, Firefly (www.fireflyz.com.my), a subsidiary of Malaysian Airlines, began operating out of Terminal 3 at **Sultan Abdul Aziz Shah Airport** (commonly known by its former name of **Subang Airport**), some 25 km out of the city centre. Firefly connect KL with Penang, Johor Bahru (JB), Langkawi, Kerteh, Koh Samui, Medan and Pekanbaru. **Berjaya Air** (www.berjaya-air.com) also uses this airport for flights to Koh Samui, Pulau Pangkor and Pulau Tioman. To get to the airport by bus, take RapidKL Bus No U81 from KL Sentral or Metro Bus No 9 from Puduraya. The nearest LRT stop is Kelana Jaya, a 15-minute taxi ride away. A taxi from the city centre will take around half an hour.

Airport departure tax is RM15 for domestic flights and RM51 for international, but this is usually included in the ticket price. ▸▸ *See Transport, page 32.*

Transport from the airport From KLIA, the **KLIA Ekspres Coach Service** ① *T03-6203 3064, www.kliaekspres.com,* provides an efficient service into the city centre to Hentian Duta (near the Tun Razak Hockey Stadium). From the KLIA Arrivals hall, go one floor down to where the coaches depart; follow the clearly marked signs. Coaches run every 30 minutes, 0500-2230 (one hour, RM25 one way). The coach goes to Hentian Duta bus station where passengers transfer to a shuttle bus (RM1) for a connection to major hotels.

The **KLIA Ekspres** ① *T03-2267 8000, www.kliaekspres.com,* runs an air-rail service every 20 minutes, 0500-2400 between the airport and **KL Central train station**. From here you can take a taxi to your hotel. The journey takes 28 minutes and costs RM35 one way. Travellers using the KLIA Ekspres can check their luggage in at KL Central for outgoing flights. Alternatively, the **KLIA Transit** ① *www.kliaekspres.com,* takes 35 minutes to make the same journey, and costs RM35. The train stops at three stations and runs 0550-0100. If your plane arrives outside these hours, take a taxi into KL or hire a car. Major car rental companies have desks in Arrivals, open 24 hours.

For a taxi expect to pay RM80-100. Taxis operate on a coupon system; collect one from the taxi counter at the exit in Arrivals (near Door 3). Touts charge more than double the official rate; bargain hard. Many hotels provide a pick-up service, but make sure they are aware of your arrival details; there is a hotel pick-up office just outside the terminal exit.

From the LCCT terminal the **Skybus** ① *www.skybus.com.my,* runs to KL Central Station. The journey takes one and a quarter hours and costs RM9. Buses depart regularly 0700-0115. If arriving on AirAsia at the LCCT, the official taxi charge to KL city centre is RM75.

24 hours in Kuala Lumpur

Begin the day by heading to the **Petronas Twin Towers**. Queue for a free ticket to the skybridge (closed Mondays) to survey the city from above. Head back to earth, pick up a copy of the *New Straits Times* and enjoying a leisurely coffee before making a foray for the classic Malay breakfast: *nasi lemak* – rice cooked in coconutmilk served with prawn sambal, ikan bilis (like anchovies), hard boiled egg and peanuts.

Head over to Chinatown and discover the two facets of Malaysia's cultural heritage: the **Sri Mahamariamman Temple** and the **Chan See Shu Yuen Temple**. For cultural balance make your way to the **Masjid Negara** (National Mosque), stopping en route at the art deco **Central Market** to browse for handicrafts.

At midday enjoy a dim sum buffet lunch, which you can work off with a walk in the 90-ha **Lake Gardens** before looking around the **Islamic Arts Museum** near its southern tip.

Next, shake off the past and witness Malaysia's tryst-with-modernity. Start the evening with a cold beer at the **Coliseum Café** before heading back to Chinatown around 1930 when the copy-watch sellers and all kinds of other hawkers emerge.

For dinner, enjoy another slice of this culinary melting pot by sampling the unique Nyonya cuisine of the Straits Malays.

While KL doesn't have the liveliest nightlife, there is still a reasonably hot stock of bars and clubs on Jalan Pinang and Jalan P Ramlee, and less touristy options in **Bangsar Baru** west of the city centre and near the university of Malaya. If your stomach grumbles after midnight, 24-hour *mamak* canteens are plentiful in **Bangsar**.

Buy a coupon from the Arrivals hall to avoid arguments. ▶▶ *For information on getting to the airport from the city, see page 32.*

Getting around

Kuala Lumpur is not the easiest city to navigate, with its sights spread thinly over a wide area. Pedestrians have not been high on the list of priorities for Malaysian urban planners, with many roads, especially outside the city centre, built without pavements, making walking both hazardous and difficult. The heavy pollution and the hot, humid climate add to the problem and, with the exception of the area around Central Market, Chinatown and Dayabumi, distances between sights are too great to cover comfortably on foot. Kuala Lumpur's bus system is labyrinthine and congested streets mean that travelling by taxi can make for a tedious wait in a traffic jam. Try to insist that taxi drivers use their meters, although don't be surprised if they refuse. The two **Light Rail Transit** (LRT), the **Monorail** and the **KMT Komuter** rail lines, are undoubtedly the least hassle and provide a great elevated and air-conditioned view of the city. The **Malaysian Tourism Centre**, see below, gives free, detailed pocket-sized maps of KL, with bus stops, monorail and LRT systems. See also www.kiat.net/malaysia/kl/transit.html.

Worth considering if short of time is the **KL Hop-on/Hop-off City Tour** ① *T03-2691 1382, www.myhoponhopoff.com, daily 0830-2030, RM38*, a hi-tech variant on the London tour bus theme. Tickets are valid for 24 hours and can be bought at hotels, travel agents and on the bus itself, which stops at 22 clearly marked points around town. A recorded commentary is available in eight languages as the bus trundles around a circuit that includes KLCC, the Golden Triangle, Petaling Street (Chinatown), KL Central Station, the National Mosque and the Palace of Culture.

Orientation

The **colonial core** is around the Padang (the cricket pitch in front of the old Selangor Club, next to Merdeka Square) and down Jalan Raja and Jalan Tun Perak. East of the Padang, straight over the bridge on Lebuh Pasar Besar, is the main commercial area, occupied by banks and finance companies. To the southeast of Merdeka Square is KL's vibrant **Chinatown**. If you get disorientated in the winding streets around **Little India** and Chinatown a good point of reference is the angular Maybank Building situated in Jalan Pudu, very close to both Puduraya Bus Terminal and Jalan Sultan. The streets to the north of the Padang are central shopping streets with modern department stores and shops.

To find a distinctively Malay area, it is necessary to venture further out, along Jalan Raja Muda Musa to **Kampong Baru**, to the northeast. To the south of Kampong Baru, on the opposite side of the Klang River, is **Jalan Ampang**, once KL's millionaires row, where tin magnates, or *towkays*, and sultans first built their homes. The road is now mainly occupied by embassies and high commissions. To the southeast of Jalan Ampang is KL's so-called **Golden Triangle**, to which the modern central business district has migrated.

Tourist information

The **Malaysian Tourism Centre (MTC)** ① *109 Jln Ampang, T03-2163 3664, daily 0700-2400,* is housed in an opulent mansion formerly belonging to a Malaysian planter and tin miner. It provides information on all 13 states, as well as money-changing facilities, an express bus ticket counter, tour reservations, a Malay restaurant, cultural shows on Tuesdays, Thursdays, Saturdays and Sundays at 1500 (RM5), demonstrations of handicrafts and a souvenir shop. There is a visitor centre on Level 3 of the airport's main terminal building.

Other useful contacts are: **Tourism Malaysia** ① *Level 2, Putra World Trade Centre, 45 Jl Tun Ismail, T03-2615 8188, T1300 885050, www.tourismmalaysia.gov.my, Mon-Fri 0900-1800;* **KL Tourist Police** ① *T03-2149 6593,* and the **Wildlife and National Parks Department** ① *Km 10, Jl Cheras, T03-9075 2872, www.wildlife.gov.my.*

Many companies offer half-day city tours, which include visits to Chinatown, the National Museum, railway station, Masjid Negara (National Mosque), the Padang area and Masjid Jamek; most cost about RM30. City night tours take in Chinatown, the Sri Mahmariamman Temple and a cultural show (RM60). Other tours visit sights close to the city such as Batu Caves, a batik factory and the Selangor Pewter Complex (RM30).

Best time to visit

The weather in KL is hot and humid all year round with temperatures rarely straying far below 20°C or much above 30°C. There is no rainy season per se, although you can get rainstorms throughout the year. Try to be here for one of the festivals (see page 11), particularly the **Thaipusam Festival**, one of the most colourful and shocking. For up-to-date weather reports, check www.kjc.gov.my.

Places in Kuala Lumpur → *For listings, see pages 27-33.*

Kuala Lumpur is a sprawling city. The big shopping malls, hip restaurants and bars are clustered around The Golden Triangle and the KLCC. Here too are the Petronas Towers, once the tallest in the world, and the Menara KL (KL Tower), another mighty spike on the landscape. The ethnic neighbourhoods lie southwest of here – there's Chinatown, a web of bustling streets filled with temples, funeral stores, restaurants and shophouses, and Little India, packed with shops selling Bollywood CDs, saris and spices. Also here is the colonial

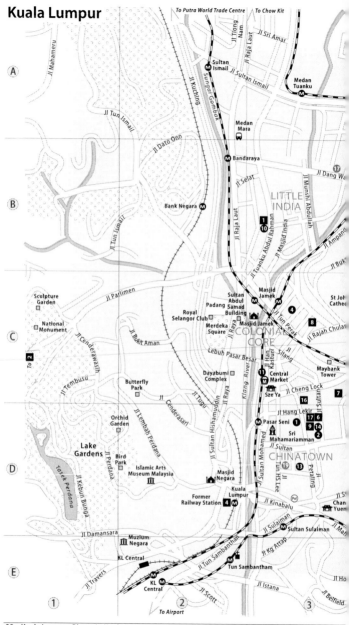

Kuala Lumpur

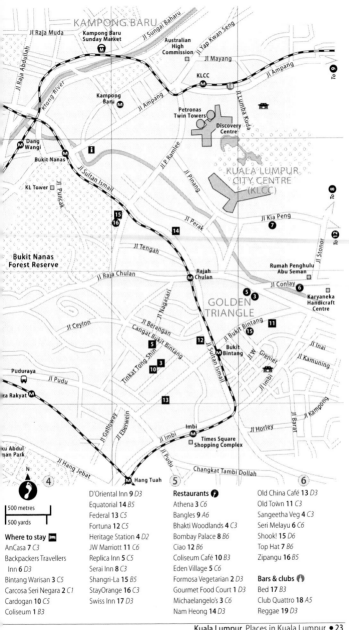

Where to stay 🛏

AnCasa 7 C3
Backpackers Travellers Inn 6 D3
Bintang Warisan 3 C5
Carcosa Seri Negara 2 C1
Cardogan 10 C5
Coliseum 1 B3
D'Oriental Inn 9 D3
Equatorial 14 B5
Federal 13 C5
Fortuna 12 C5
Heritage Station 4 D2
JW Marriott 11 C6
Replica Inn 5 C5
Serai Inn 8 C3
Shangri-La 15 B5
StayOrange 16 C3
Swiss Inn 17 D3

Restaurants 🍴

Athena 3 C6
Bangles 9 A6
Bhakti Woodlands 4 C3
Bombay Palace 8 B6
Ciao 12 B6
Coliseum Café 10 B3
Eden Village 5 C6
Formosa Vegetarian 2 D3
Gourmet Food Court 1 D3
Michaelangelo's 3 C6
Nam Heong 14 D3

Old China Café 13 D3
Old Town 11 C3
Sangeetha Veg 4 C3
Seri Melayu 6 C6
Shook! 15 D6
Top Hat 7 B6
Zipangu 16 B5

Bars & clubs 🍸

Bed 17 B3
Club Quattro 18 A5
Reggae 19 D3

core where the remnants of the British empire line Merdeka Square. You can escape from the hustle a few streets southwest of here in the Lake Gardens, which house the fine Islamic Arts Museum and a bird and orchid park.

Colonial core and Little India

Behind the Masjid Jamek mosque (see below), from the corner of Jalan Tuanku Abdul Rahman and Jalan Raja Laut, are the colonial-built public buildings, distinguished by their grand Moorish architecture. The **Sultan Abdul Samad Building**, with its distinctive clocktower and bulbous copper domes, houses the **Supreme Court**.

The Sultan Abdul Samad Building faces on to the Padang on the opposite side of the road, next to **Merdeka Square**. The old Selangor Club cricket pitch is the venue for **Independence Day** celebrations. The centrepiece of Merdeka Square is the tallest flagpole in the world (100 m high) and the huge Malaysian flag that flies from the top can be seen across half the city, particularly at night when it is floodlit.

South of the Masjid Jamek mosque, on Jalan Raya, is the 35-storey, marble **Dayabumi Complex**, one of KL's most striking landmarks. It was designed by local architect Datuk Nik Mohamed and introduces contemporary Islamic architecture to the skyscraper era.

On the opposite bank to the Dayabumi Complex is the **Central Market** ⓘ *www. centralmarket.com.my*, a former wet market built in 1928 in art deco style, tempered with local baroque trimmings. In the early 1980s it was revamped to become a focus for KL's artistic community. It is a warren of boutiques, handicraft and souvenir stalls, some with their wares laid out on the wet market's original marble slabs.

Northwest of the old railway station is the **Masjid Negara (National Mosque)** ⓘ *Sat-Thu 0900-1800, Fri 1445-1800, Muslims can visit the mosque 0630-2200, women must use a separate entrance*, the modern spiritual centre of KL's Malay population and the symbol of Islam for the whole country. Completed in 1965, it occupies a 5-ha site at the end of Jalan Hishamuddin. Close to the National Mosque is the **Islamic Arts Museum Malaysia** ⓘ *Jl Lembah Perdana, T03-2274 2020, www.iamm.org.my, daily 1000-1800, RM12*, which provides a fascinating collection of textiles and metalware from diverse areas such as Iran, India, South Asia and China. It's a wonderful oasis in the midst of the city.

Little India's streets – Jalan Masjid India and nearby lanes – resonate to the sounds of Bollywood CDs and hawker cries. There are stalls and stores selling garish gold, saris, fabrics, great *kurta* (pyjama smocks), traditional medicines, flowers and spices. It is also a good place to eat cheap Indian snacks and sip on sweet lassis. Although the streets are fairly scruffy, the smells and colours make up for its lack of gloss.

At the muddy confluence of the Klang and Gombak rivers where KL's founders stepped ashore stands the **Masjid Jamek** ⓘ *entrance on Jalan Tun Perak, daily 0900-1100, 1400-1600*, formerly the National Mosque. Built in 1909 by English architect, AB Hubbock, the mosque has a walled courtyard (*sahn*) and a three-domed prayer hall. It is striking with its striped white and salmon-coloured brickwork and domed minarets, cupolas and arches.

Chinatown

Southeast of the Central Market, Chinatown is bounded by Jalan Tun HS Lee (Jalan Bandar), Jalan Petaling and Jalan Sultan. A mixture of crumbling shophouses, coffee shops and restaurants, this quarter wakes up during late afternoon, when its streets become the centre of frenetic trading and haggling. Jalan Petaling and parts of Jalan Sultan are transformed into an open-air night market (*pasar malam*). Food stalls selling Chinese, Indian and Malay delicacies, and all manner of impromptu boutiques line the streets.

The extravagantly decorated **Sri Mahamariamman Temple** is south of Jalan Hang Lekir, tucked away on Jalan Tun HS Lee (Jalan Bandar). Incorporating gold, precious stones and Spanish and Italian tiles, it was founded in 1873 by Tamils from South India who had come to Malaya as contract labourers to work in the rubber plantations or on the roads and railways. It has a silver chariot dedicated to Lord Murugan (Subramaniam), which is taken in procession to the Batu Caves during the Thaipusam Festival (see page 11).

The elaborate Chinese **Chan See Shu Yuen Temple**, at the southern end of Jalan Petaling, was built in 1906 and has a typical open courtyard and symmetrical pavilions. Paintings, woodcarvings and ceramic sculptures decorate the facade. Ornate clan houses (*kongsis*) can be seen nearby; a typical one is near the **Chan Kongsi** on Jalan Maharajalela.

Lake Gardens and around

ⓘ *Bus 21C or 48C from Kotaraya Plaza, or bus 18 or 21A from Chow Kit; alight at old train station.*
Near the southern tip of the Lake Gardens, is the **Muzium Negara** ⓘ *T03-2282 6255, www. museum.gov.my, daily 0900-1800, RM2*, with its Minangkabau-style roof and two large murals of Italian glass mosaic on either side of the main entrance. They depict the main historical episodes and cultural activities of Malaysia. The museum provides an excellent introduction to Malaysia's history, geography, natural history and culture.

Close to the museum is the south entrance to the 90-ha **Lake Gardens**. Pedal boats can be hired at the weekend. The gardens also house a hibiscus garden, orchid garden and sculpture garden; as well as children's playgrounds, picnic areas, restaurants and cafés, and a small deer park. At the north end of the Lake Gardens is the **National Monument**. This 15-m memorial provides a good view of Parliament House.

The showpiece of the Lake Gardens is the **Bird Park** ⓘ *www.birdpark.com.my, daily 0900-1900, RM28*. The world's largest covered bird park, it houses more than 2000 birds from 200 species, ranging from ducks to hornbills.

The **Butterfly Park** ⓘ *daily 0900-1800, RM17*, is a miniature jungle, which is home to almost 8000 butterflies from 150 species. There are also small mammals, amphibians and reptiles and rare tropical insects in the park.

Kuala Lumpur City Centre (KLCC)

This area has been the focus of extraordinary redevelopment and is known as the **Kuala Lumpur City Centre (KLCC)** ⓘ *www.klcc.com.my*, a city within a city. The complex is one of the largest real estate developments in the world, covering a 40-ha site and including the Petronas Towers. The city's offices, hotels and shopping complexes are mostly concentrated in the Golden Triangle, see below, on the east side of the city.

The **Petronas Twin Towers** were designed by American architect Cesar Pelli and the surrounding park by the Brazilian landscape artist Roberto Marx Burle. The **Sky Bridge** ⓘ *T03-2331 8080, Tue-Sun 0900-1900*, links the two towers on the 41st floor. Visitors must queue for a first-come first-served ticket that gives free access to the bridge and stunning views. Only a limited number of people are allowed up every day, so it is advisable to get there before 1000, especially on weekends. The **Discovery Centre** ⓘ *Level 4, Suria KLCC Petrosains, T03-2331 8181, Sat and Sun 0930-1830, Tue, Wed, Thu 0930-1730, Fri 1330-1730, RM12*, has rides and hands-on computer games glorifying the petroleum industry but is a great place for children.

Menara KL and the Bukit Nanas Forest Reserve

ⓘ *T03-2020 5448 for reservations, www.menarakl.com.my. Daily 0900-2200. RM20. There is no public transport, so take a taxi or walk from one of the nearby roads.*

Near the intersection of Jalan Ampang and Jalan Sultan Ismail atop Bukit Nanas stands the **Menara KL** (KL Tower). This 421-m-high tower is the fourth tallest in the world (the viewing platform stands at 276 m). The tower is the brainchild of former prime minister Dr Mahathir Mohammed. The views from the top on a clear day are superb, much better than those from the Skybridge at the Petronas Twin Towers. At ground level are several shops, fast-food restaurants and a mini amphitheatre. Above the viewing platform is the **Seri Angkasa** revolving restaurant.

Combine a visit to the tower with a walk in the **Bukit Nanas Forest Reserve** ⓘ *free, a* beautiful 11-ha area of woodland in the city centre with marked trails. KL is perhaps the only city with a patch of rainforest at its heart. Butterflies, monkeys and birds live here.

Golden Triangle

The **Rumah Penghulu Abu Seman** ⓘ *Jln Stonor, T03-2162 7459, Mon-Sat 1000-1700, tours of the centre start at 1100 and 1500, RM5*, otherwise known as the **Heritage Centre of the Badan Warisan Malaysia**, is in a mock-Tudor building off Jalan Conloy, on the northern edge of the Golden Triangle. In the garden is a reconstructed headman's house made of timber displaying detailed carvings and furnished in the style of a 1930s house. Just to the east of the Heritage Centre is the **Komplex Budaya Kraf**, a handicraft centre offering you the chance to watch artists at work.

One of the newest shopping plazas in the Golden Triangle is **Times Square** on Jalan Imbi, with a rollercoaster, Imax cinema, shops, hotel and restaurants.

Around Kuala Lumpur

The most popular day trip is to the **Batu Caves** ⓘ *13 km north, open until 2100, RM1 taxi (30 mins) or bus No 11 or 11D (1 hr) from Central Market*, which is a fun day out. This series of caverns is reached by a sweat-inducing flight of 272 steps with colourful Hindu paraphernalia. Set high in a massive limestone outcrop, the caves were discovered by American naturalist William Hornaby in the 1880s. In 1891 Hindu priests set up a shrine in the main cave dedicated to Lord Muraga and it has now become the biggest Indian pilgrimage centre in Malaysia during the Thaipusam Festival (see page 11), when 800,000 Hindus congregate.

Kuala Selangor Nature Park ⓘ *T03-3289 2294, www.mns.org.my, RM4, buses from KL's Puduraya bus terminal to Kuala Selangor, then taxi 8 km to Kampong Kuantan, boat trips from Kampong Kuantan cost RM10 each or RM40 to charter*, consists of 250 ha of coastal mangrove swamp and wetland. It has several observation hides, 156 bird species (including bee eaters, kingfishers and sea eagles) and leaf monkeys. It is also one of the best places to see Malaysia's famous synchronized fireflies – the only fireflies in Southeast Asia that coordinate their flashing; they are best observed on a moonless night, from about one hour after sunset. There are various trails, a mangrove walk and a visitor centre (daily 0900-1800). It's possible to stay overnight at the centre; accommodation includes A-frame huts, chalets and dorms and should be booked in advance. Hotels and guesthouse offer day trips to see the fireflies with prices starting at RM160.

Kuala Lumpur listings

For hotel and restaurant price codes and other relevant information, see pages 9-11.

🍽 Where to stay

Most top hotels are between Jln Sultan Ismail and Jln P Ramlee, in KL's Golden Triangle. South of Jln Raja Chulan, in the Bukit Bintang area, there is another concentration of big hotels. Many reduce their room rates Mon-Fri.

There are also lots of cheap hotels in the Golden Triangle and along Jl Bukit Bintang. Chinatown is home to rock-bottom budget places, some of which are rather run-down, others are tailor-made backpacker hostels.

Many of the cheaper hotels are around Jln Tuanku Abdul Rahman, Jln Masjid India and Jln Raja Laut, all of which are within easy walking distance of the colonial core of KL (although these tend to be quite sleazy and run down), northeast of the Padang.

Colonial core and Little India
p24, map p22

$ Coliseum, 100 Jln Tuanku Abdul Rahman, T03-2692 6270. For those on a budget who want a taste of the 1920s. Large, simple rooms with fans or a/c, shared bathrooms. Rooms facing the main street are noisy. Famous bar and restaurant (see page 29), friendly.

Chinatown *p24, map p22*

$$$ AnCasa, Jln Cheng Lock, next to Puduraya bus station, T03-2026 6060, www.ancasa-hotel.com. Well-furnished, clean a/c rooms with TV, internet, minibar and safe. Restaurant and bar. Breakfast included. Walking tours of KL available and homestay programme in a variety of locations can be organized here. Recommended.

$$$ Swiss Inn, 62 Jln Sultan, T03-2072 3333, www.swissgarden.com. Fair value lodgings in the heart of Chinatown.

Rooms in the new wing are a little on the small side, but feature flatscreen TV, good mattress and new, spotless bathroom. Rooms in the older wing come without windowns. Free internet access (no Wi-Fi), breakfast included.

$$ D'Oriental Inn, 82 Jln Petaling, T03-2026 8181, www.dorientalinn.com. Newly renovated hotel with a selection of clean, well-furnished a/c rooms with attached bathroom and free Wi-Fi access in all rooms. Friendly staff. Recommended.

$$ Serai Inn, Jln Hang Lekiu, T03-2070 4728, www.seraiinn.com. Rooms here are tiny with paper thin walls, but are kept spotless and all have free Wi-Fi access. Bathrooms are shared, but kept very clean. Rooftop terrace for smokers, and communal area with TV, internet access and free tea and coffee all day. Recommended.

$$ Stay Orange Hotel, 16 Jln Petaling, T03-2070 2208, www.stayorange.com. Somewhat akin to living inside an EasyJet 737, the bright orange walls and branding can be a tad off-putting, but rooms here are spotless and feature free Wi-Fi, a/c and good bedding. Book online in advance for excellent rates.

$$-$ Backpackers Travellers Inn, 2nd floor, 60 Jln Sultan, T03-238 2473, www.backpackers kl.com. Well-run hotel with attached travel agency and relaxed rooftop bar/café with good views and cheap beer. Rooms are simple and the owner is proactive in the fight against bugs, with each room having bug deterrents and seamless mattress covers. Rooms are small, dark and unattractive but generally clean, ranging from a/c dorm rooms (RM 11 per night) to single windowless fan rooms or a/c rooms with attached showers. Good facilities for the traveller including left luggage, washing and cooking facilities. Also has book exchange, video, television and laundry. Wi-Fi access (RM5 per day).

$$-$ Heritage Station, Banguanan Stesen Keretapi, Jln Sultan Hishamuddin, T03-2272 1688, www.heritagehotelmalaysia.com. Part of the magnificent Moorish-style railway station. It has retained some of its colonial splendour, but the rooms are furnished in a contemporary style. Cranky lifts, saggy floors and lukewarm food, but unbeatable for atmosphere and location. Also backpacker dorms in a/c rooms with their own bathroom. Wi-Fi in lobby.

Lake Gardens and around
p25, map p22

$$$$ Carcosa Seri Negara, Taman Tasek Perdana, T03-2282 1888, www.ghmhotels.com. Former residence of the British High Commissioner built in 1896 and now a high-class hotel where important dignitaries, presidents and prime ministers are pampered on state visits. Set in a secluded wooded hillside overlooking the Lake Gardens. A/c, restaurant, pool.

KLCC *p25, map p22*

$$$$ Shangri-La, 11 Jln Sultan Ismail, T03-2032 2388, www.shangri-la.com. With its grand marble lobby and 720 rooms, the 'Shang' remains KL's ritziest hotel. It plays host to political leaders and assorted royalty for dinner. The best feature is its ground floor **Gourmet Corner** deli, which stocks a great variety of European food. A/c, small, rather old-fashioned pool, health club, sauna, jacuzzi, tennis.

$$$$-$$$ Equatorial, Jln Sultan Ismail, T03-2161 7777, www.equatorial.com. One of KL's earlier international hotels. Its 1960s-style coffee shop has become one of the best in town, open 24 hrs. With an international news agency in the basement. A/c, restaurant (excellent Cantonese), pool. Rooms at the back get less traffic noise.

Golden Triangle *p26, map p22*

$$$$ Federal, 35 Jln Bukit Bintang, T03-2148 9166, www.federal.com.my. Once glam, but now looking a tad old school, this hotel has spacious a/c rooms with internet access and cable TV. Indian fun pub and Irish pub, revolving restaurant on 18th floor, ice cream bar, cafés, bowling, shopping arcade, business centre, pool. When it opened in the early 1960s it was the pride of KL: its **Mandarin Palace** restaurant was once rated as the most elegant restaurant in the Far East, and is still good, but does not compare with the world-class glitz in contemporary KL.

$$$$ JW Marriott, 183 Jln Bukit Bintang, T03-2715 9000, www.marriott.com. Next to **Star Hill** shopping mall, has pool, fitness centre, conference facilities. Magnificent in its extravagance.

$$$ Fortuna, 87 Jln Berangan, T03-2141 9111, www.fortunakl.com. Tucked away just off Bukit Bintang. Slightly quieter than most and good value for money. A/c, health centre, coffee house with live music. Recommended.

$$ Bintang Warisan, 68 Jln Bukit Bintang, T03-2148 8111, www.bintangwarisan.com. Well-managed hotel with clean, spacious a/c room with TV and attached bathroom. Most rooms have windows; some have their own gardens. Some rooms have excellent views of the Twin Towers.

$$ Cardogan, 64 Jln Bukit Bintang, T03-2144 4883. Rooms (all a/c) are simple and clean but a little old with small attached white-tiled bathroom. Coffee house, health centre, business centre.

$$ Replica Inn, Changay Bukit Bintang, T03-2142 1771, www.replicainn.com. Newish place in a super location for shops and food stalls, rooms here are excellent value with good bedding, TV and attached bathroom. There's a good Malay café downstairs. Another branch on Jln Petaling in Chinatown.

❼ Restaurants

Many of KL's big hotels in the **Jln Sultan Ismail/Bukit Bintang** areas serve excellent-value buffet lunches. **Cangkat Bukit Bintang** and **Tingkat Tong Shin** streets, west of Jln Bukit Bintang are the latest trendy eating areas.

Food stalls
The best area is **Chow Kit**. On Jln Raja Muda Abdul Aziz there is a food court with great Indian and Afghan food. Jln Haji Hussien has a collection of superb food stalls. Walk up Jln Haji Hussien and turn right. The food court on the top floor of **The Mall** is run down but has an attractive ambience. The Indian, Malay and Chinese choices are all good, but the majority close by 2000. It's cheap too – tandoori chicken, naan, dhal and a drink cost just RM8. Jln Raja Alang and Jln Raja Bot stalls, off Jln Tuanku Abdul Rahman, are mostly Malay. **Kampong Baru** and **Kampong Datok Keramat** are Malay communities. On the riverfront behind Jln Mesjid India are good Indian and Malay night stalls. Jln Masjid India, **Little India**, has many good Indian and Malay foodstalls. **Sunday Market**, Kampong Baru (main market actually takes place on Sat night), has many Malay hawker stalls. For lovers of Chinese and Malay food, noodle bars and deep fried delights, you'll find the Chinatown markets on Jln Sultan, Jln Tun HS Lee and Petaling St very rewarding.

Colonial core and Little India
p24, map p22
$$ Coliseum Café, 100 Jln Tuanku Abdul Rahman (Batu Rd). Famed for its sizzling lamb and beef steaks, Hainanese (Chinese) food and Western-style (mild) curries. During the Communist Emergency, planters were said to come here for gin and curry, handing their guns in to be kept behind the bar.
$ Bhakti Woodlands, 55 Leboh Ampang, T03-2034 2399. Open 0900-1000. Good selection of vegetarian Indian food with

set lunches, tasty masala dosai and lashings of sugary tea.
$ Sangeetha Veg Restaurant, 65 Jln Lebuh Ampang, T03-2032 3333. Open 1100-2230. With branches all over India, this tidy restaurant is a great place to sample some true Indian veg fare (including Jain) in a/c comfort. The thalis (most served 1100-1500) are truly gargantuan, and the *papad* are deliciously peppery. Recommended.

Chinatown *p24, map p22*
$$ Old China Café, 11 Jln Balai Polis, T03-2072 5915, www.oldchina.com.my. Interesting Nyonya and Malay favourites, including *asam* prawns (prawns cooked with candlenuts and tamarind), *mee siam* and plenty of seafood dishes. The walls are covered in old photos of Malaysia and the tables are topped with marble. Lots of olde worlde ambience. Fine choice for a romantic evening out.
$ Formosa Vegetarian, 48 Jln Sultan. Huge menu of fake meats and fish, beancurds and other creative veggie dishes.
$ Gourmet Food Court, Jln Petaling, opposite **The Swiss Inn**. A great vegetarian counter with a dozen choices of tasty vegetables and beancurd to pile on rice. Best cheap breakfast in Chinatown.
$ Nam Heong, 54 Jln Sultan. Open 1000-1500. Clean and non fussy place specializing in delightful plates of delicious Hainanese chicken rice, but also featuring some wonderful Chinese delights including pork with yam (truly outstanding), *asam* fish and fresh tofu.
$ Old Town, G/F Central Market, www.old town.com.my. With a menu of simple kopitiam fare, this place is jammed at breakfast with locals hunting out the thick *kaya* toast with butter, dark thick coffee and well-priced meals.

Lake Gardens and around
p25, map p22
$$$ Carcosa Seri Negara, see Where to stay. Served in a sumptuous, colonial setting,

English-style high tea (recommended), expensive Italian lunches and dinners are also served in the Mahsuri dining hall on fine china plates with solid silver cutlery.

KLCC *p25, map p22*

$$$ Ciao, 428 Jln Tun Razak, T03-9285 4827. Tue-Sun 1200-1430, 1900-2230. Authentic, tasty Italian food served in a beautifully renovated bungalow.

$$ Bangles, 270 Jln Ampang, T03-4532 4100. Reckoned to be among the best North Indian tandoori restaurants in KL. It's often necessary to book in the evenings.

$$ Bombay Palace, 215 Jln Tun Razak, T03-2145 4241. Good-quality North Indian food in tasteful surroundings with staff in traditional Indian uniform. Menu includes vegetarian section. Winners of the Malaysian Tourism Award for several years.

$$ Seri Melayu, 1 Jln Conlay, T03-2145 1833, www.serimelayu.com. Open 1100-1500, 1900-2300. One of the best Malay restaurants in town in a traditional Minangkabau-style building. Beautifully designed interior. Don't be put off by cultural shows or big groups – the food is superb and amazingly varied; it's very popular with locals too. Individual dishes are expensive, the buffet is the best bet (more than 50 dishes), with promotions featuring cuisine from different states each month. Those arriving in shorts will be given a sarong.

$$ Top Hat, 7 Jln Kia Peng, T03-2241 3611. Good eastern Nyonya set menu, some Western dishes. Set in a 1930s colonial bungalow, just south of KLCC.

Golden Triangle *p26, map p22*

The basement of the **Pavillion Mall** has one of the city's best (and most expensive) food courts with a wonderful variety of food including Vietnamese, Thai, Japanese, Indonesian and Malay. A meal costs around RM10. There are also a number of other good-value restaurants in the basement.

$$$ Shook!, The Feast Floor, Starhill Gallery, Jln Bukit Bintang, T03-2719 8535.

Emphasizing seasonal trends, the fusion menu includes Japanese, Chinese, Italian and a Western grill. Popular with celebrities and featuring a huge walk-in wine cellar with over 3000 bottles.

$$$ Zipangu, Shangri-La Hotel, 11 Jln Sultan Ismail, T03-2032 2388. Regular winner of best restaurant, with a small Japanese garden. Limited menu but highly regarded.

$$ Athena, Pavilion Mall, T03-2141 5131. The bright blue and white decor screams Greece and while there are a few Greek dishes on the menu, there is evidence of other Western cusines in dishes such as nutmeg fish fillet.

$$ Eden Village, 260 Jln Raja Chulan. Wide-ranging menu, but probably best known for seafood. Resembles a glitzy Minangkabau palace with a garden behind. Cultural Malay, Chinese and Indian dances every night.

$$ Michelangelo's, Pavilion Mall, T03-2141 1123. Open 0900-0100. While the atmosphere is a tad sterile, the portions in this Italian joint are good with a menu that sweeps effortlessly from superb seafood, perfect pizza and knotted spaghetti.

Teahouses

Try out the Chinese teahouse opposite the **Sungai Wang Hotel** on Jln Bukit Bintang.

🔾 Bars and clubs

Kuala Lumpur *p18, map p22*

Kuala Lumpur has a vibrant bar scene. Several streets have emerged over the past 5 years or so as hip scenes to be seen in. The **Golden Triangle** is a good place to find bars and clubs especially in the main bar and club street, Jln P Ramlee, but a few bars have begun setting up in **Cangkat Bukit Bintang**, and this area is set to grow more popular. **Bangsar** and **Desi Sri Hartamas** are 2 areas just outside the centre of KL that have developed into popular nightlife spots. Bars, restaurants, coffee shops and *mamaks* stand side by side in a network of streets in both these areas. Most venues stay open until the early hours.

See the 'Metro' section in *The Star* (Malaysia's most widely read English-language daily) for what's on. Also check out freebie magazines such as *Juice* (available in bars and clubs) or *KL lifestyle*, *KLUE* and *KL Vision* (usually free in hotels; if not, they are available in newsagents for about RM5).

Night-time on the streets around Chinatown is pretty busy and there are plenty of bars offering cheap beer.
Bed, Heritage Row, 33 Jln Yap Ah Shak, T03-2693 1122, www.bed.com.my. Trying hard to attract the beautiful people, beds are scattered around this venue for the suave and sophisticated to lounge to a backdrop of laid-back contemporary tunes.
Club Quattro, G/F Avenue K, Jln Ampang, www.clubquattro.com. Tries to encompass the atmosphere of 4 seasons into its club with an icy **Winter Bar** and comedy in the **Spring Bar**, this place is loaded with gimmicks but makes for a fun night out.
Reggae Bar, 158 Jln Tun HS Lee, below **Backpackers Travellers Lodge**, Chinatown. Offers the standard mix of Bob Marley music, cheap drinks and reasonable food. Occasional big screen football matches.
Zouk, 113 Jln Ampang, T03-2171 1997, www.zoukclub.com.my. Perhaps KL's longest-running fashionable nightclub. A glowing domed exterior with changing hue encapsulates the groovy interior. Occasional gay parties, R&B and mambo evenings with Fri showcases of top international DJs such as Tiesto and Armin Van Buuren. Also has one of KL's coolest bars, **Velvet Underground**, playing a selection of commercial classics at weekends. Ladies free admission plus 5 free drinks on Tue. Smart dress code, over 21s only. Recommended.

🎭 Entertainment

Kuala Lumpur *p18, map p22*
Cultural shows
Central Market, T03-2274 6542. Weekends at 1945, performances of Chinese Opera, Bangsawan (Malay Traditional Theatre) and Nadagam (Indian Traditional Theatre).
Temple of Fine Arts, 116 Jln Berhala, Brickfields, T03-2274 3709, www.templeof finearts.org. This organization, set up in Malaysia to preserve and promote Indian culture, stages cultural shows every month with dinner, music and dancing. The temple organizes an annual **Festival of Arts**, which involves a week of traditional and modern Indian dance. It also runs classes in classical and folk dancing.

🛍 Shopping

Kuala Lumpur *p18, map p22*
Many of the handicrafts are imported from Indonesia. The areas to look for Chinese arts and handicrafts are along Jln Tuanku Abdul Rahman and in the centre of Bangsar. Jln Masjid India, running parallel with Jln Tuanku Abdul Rahman, is a treasure trove of all things Indian, from saris to sandalwood oil, bangles to brass incense burners. For clothes, shoes, bags and textiles try Jln Sultan and Jln Tun HS Lee, close to Klang bus station. In Petaling St, **Chinatown**, you can barter for Chinese lanterns, paintings and incense holders.
Batik Corner, Lot L1.13, Weld Shopping Centre, 76 Jln Raja Chulan. Excellent selection of sarong lengths and ready-mades in batiks from all over Malaysia and Indonesia.
Central Market, Jln Hang Kasturi. A purpose-built area with 2 floors of boutiques and craft stalls including pewter, jewellery, jade, wood and ceramics. Stalls of note include one that sells all kinds of moulds and cutters for baking, a wonderful spice stall, another one for nuts and for dried fruits. Downstairs are hand-painted silk batik scarves and sarongs.

Faeroes, Weld Shopping Centre, Jln Raja Chulan (also at 42B Jln Nirvana, just off Jln Tun Ismail). Exclusive and original batiks. Recommended.

Jln Melayu. An interesting area for browsing, with its Indian shops filled with silk saris and brass pots and Malay outlets specializing in Islamic paraphernalia such as *songkok* (velvet Malay hats) and prayer rugs as well as herbal medicines and oils.

Jln Tuanku Abdul Rahman, Batu Rd. This was KL's best shopping street for decades and is transformed weekly into a pedestrian mall and night market every Sat 1700-2200.

Kampong Baru Sunday Market (Pasar Mange), off Jln Raja Muda Musa (a large Malay enclave at the north end of KL). This open-air market comes alive on Sat nights, when a variety of stalls selling batik sarongs, bamboo birdcages and traditional handicrafts compete with dozens of food stalls. However, the Pasar Mange has largely been superseded by Central Market as a place to buy handicrafts.

Pertama Shopping Complex, Jln Abdul Tunku Abdul Rahman. In the Chow Kit area near the Bandaraya LRT station. A great place for bargain hunters, with a wide range of products from souvenirs to fashion, photographic/electronic goods. KL's original department store.

Suria KLCC. This vast shopping complex is great for a Western splurge, with most designer brands you'd expect; however, don't expect prices to be much lower than in Europe or North America. A good find is **Kinokuniya Book Store** on Level 4, which has one the best ranges of English-language books in Southeast Asia. On level 1, **Royal Selangor Pewter** has been recommended for luxury gifts.

☸ What to do

Kuala Lumpur *p18, map p22*
Asian Trails, Sdn Bhd 11-2-B Jln Manau, off Jln Kg Attap 50460, T03-2274 9488, www.asiantrails.info.

☐ Transport

Kuala Lumpur *p18, map p22*
Air
KL's international airport is at Sepang; see page 19 for airport information and details of transport to the city.

For a taxi from the city to KL Airport (1 hr) expect to pay RM70-90 when you buy a coupon. Hotels can arrange a good fare at around RM75. Make sure the taxi fare includes the motorway toll for either direction. Taxis to LCCT for **AirAsia** flights charge similar prices. **Skybus** services to LCCT leave from KL Sentral (9RM, 1 hr 45 mins) and runs from 0330 until 2200; however, taking a shared taxi is probably the easiest and most painless way.

Bus
The network is run by **RapidKL**, T03-7625 6999, www.rapidkl.com.my. All RapidKL bus tickets offer unlimited daily bus transport – excellent value. See their website for details of routes and timetables.

Car hire
Companies have desks at the airport terminal. Arrange a hotel pick-up service in advance or at the office outside the terminal.

Taxi
KL is one of the cheaper cities in Southeast Asia for taxis and there are stands all over town, but you can hail a taxi pretty much anywhere you like. Most are a/c and metered, but it is a challenge sometimes to get the driver to use the meter: RM2 for the 1st 2 km and RM0.10 for every 150 m thereafter. Extra charges apply 2400-0600 (50% surcharge), for each extra passenger in excess of 2, as well as RM1 for luggage in the boot. Waiting charges are RM2 for the 1st 2 mins and RM0.10 for every subsequent 45 seconds. During rush hours, shift change (around 1500) or if it's raining, it can be very difficult to persuade taxis to travel to the centre of town; negotiate a price (locals

claim that waving a RM10 bill helps) or jump in and feign ignorance. For a 24-hr taxi service try the following: **Comfort**, T03-2692 2525; **KL Taxi**, T03-9221 4241; **Teletaxi**, T03-9221 1011. 1 RM charge for phone bookings. Pre-paid voucher taxi system available at KTM KL Station, KLIA, KL Sentral.

Train

Within the city there are 5 rail systems: 2 **LRT** lines, the Ampang (yellow) and Sri Petaling (light green) and Kelana Jaya (dark green); 2 **KTM Komuter** lines (blue and red), and the **monorail** (light blue). Trains leave every 5-15 mins, and tickets cost upwards of RM0.70. Going from one line to the other often means coming out of the station and crossing a road. All lines except the **Sri Petaling** and the **Kelana Jaya** lines go through KL Central. The trains are a great way to see the city as they mostly run on elevated rails, 10 m above street level. LRT lines are run by **RapidKL**. For details of fares, routes and timetables, call T03-7625 6999 or visit www.rapidkl.com.my. **KTMB** operates commuter lines, T03-2267 1200, www.ktmb.com.my. For monorail information, see www.monorail.com.my.

ⓘ Directory

Kuala Lumpur *p18, map p22*
Banks Money changers are in all the big shopping centres and along the main shopping streets and give better rates than banks. Most branches of the leading Malaysian and foreign banks have foreign exchange desks, although some (for example, **Bank Bumiputra**) impose limits on charge card cash advances. There are ATMs everywhere for Cirrus, Visa, MasterCard, Maestro or Plus cards. **American Express**, 18th floor, The Weld (near KL Tower), Jln Raja Chulan, T03-2050 0000. **Embassies and consulates** Australia, 6 Jln Yap Kwan Seng, T03-2146 5555, www.australia.org. my. Canada, 17th floor, Menara Tan & Tan, 207 Jln Tun Razak, T03-2718 3333, www. international.gc.ca/missions/malaysia-malaisie. France, 192-196 Jln Ampang, T03-2162 0671, www.ambafrance-my.org. Germany, 26th Floor, Menara Tan & Tan, 207, Jln Tun Razak, T03-2170 9666, www. german-embassy.org.my. Indonesia, 233 Jln Tun Razak, T03-242 1354, www.kbrikl. org.my. Netherlands, Suite 7.01, 7th floor, The Ampblock, 218 Jln Ampang, T03-2168 6200, www.netherlands.org.my. New Zealand, 21st floor, Menara IMC, Jln Sultan Ismail, T03-2078 2533, www.nzembassy. com. UK, 185 Jln Ampang, T03-2148 2122, www.britain.org.my. USA, 376 Jln Tun Razak, T03-2168 5000, www.malaysia.usembassy. gov. **Emergencies** Fire: T994. Police/ambulance: T999. **Internet** Internet cafés are everywhere, many open 24 hrs. There are dozens along Jln Bukit Bintang and a few around Chinatown. Expect to pay upwards of RM3 per hr. If you're travelling with a laptop, buy a drink at an upmarket hotel bar or café – like **Starbucks** – and you'll usually get free Wi-Fi. **Medical services** Casualty wards are open 24 hrs. Gleneagles Hospital, 282-286 Jln Ampang, T03-4257 1300, www.gimc. com.my. Pantai Medical Centre, T03-2296 0888, www.pantai.com.my. Pudu Specialist Centre, Jln Baba, T03-2142 9146. Tung Shin Hospital, 102 Jln Pudu, T03-2072 1655.

Contents

Footprint features

Malaysian Peninsula

Northern Peninsula

North of KL are the temperate hill resorts and tea plantations of the Cameron Highlands, reminiscent of the English countryside and a popular weekend retreat. The former tin-rush town of Ipoh offers Straits Chinese architecture and some superb food. It is off the beaten track for many tourists, so makes a welcome break from the travel network. Offshore there is the 25-km-long island of Penang with its fine capital Georgetown packed with Chinese shophouses, temples and clan houses, and an array of beachside hotels. Less developed are the islands of Pulau Pangkor to the south and Pulau Langkawi to the north. The latter is closer to Thailand than to mainland Malaysia and offers world-class resorts, fine beaches and jungle adventures.

Cameron Highlands → *For listings, see pages 48–62.*

The biggest and best known of Malaysia's hill stations lies on a jungle-clad 1500-m-high plateau. The hills and forests provide excellent opportunities for walking, and the fertile conditions make it an important farming area. There are three main townships: **Ringlet**, famous for its tea plantations, **Tanah Rata**, the main town with shops, hotels and restaurants, and **Brinchang**, with its temples, rose gardens and strawberry farms. In recent years, the highlands have lost some of their charm with the development of golf courses and luxury resorts, but visitors still flock here to escape the heat and enjoy the peaceful surroundings. The weather is reassuringly British – unpredictable, often wet and decidedly cool – but when the sun blazes the Camerons are hard to beat.

Visiting the Cameron Highlands
Getting there and around Buses run from KL's Puduraya terminal and Georgetown direct to the Cameron Highlands. Alternatively catch a bus or train to Tapah, from where local buses run every two hours to Tanah Rata and Brinchang. A highway links Ipoh to the Cameron Highlands and runs to Gua Musang for connections to the east coast. Getting around is easiest if you have your own car, however there are local buses and taxis.

Best time to visit Due to their altitude, the highland resorts are a good escape from the heat of the plains all year round. However, it might be worth avoiding it during school and public holidays when it gets very crowded. It gets chilly at night, so bring warm clothes.

Tourist information There is no official tourist office but information can be obtained from backpacker guesthouses and tour agencies in Tanah Rata. **Golden Highlands Adventure Holidays** ① *T05-490 1880, www.gohighadventure.com*, has an office in the bus station and offers tours of the area including forest treks and visits to tea plantations,

Cameron Highlands

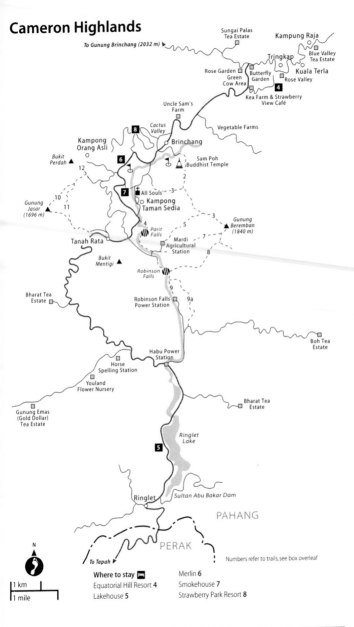

To Gunung Brinchang (2032 m) ►

Sungai Palas Tea Estate

Kampung Raja

Tringkap

Blue Valley Tea Estate

Kuala Terla

Rose Garden
Green Cow Area

Butterfly Garden

Rose Valley

4

Kea Farm & Strawberry View Café

Uncle Sam's Farm

Vegetable Farms

Cactus Valley

8

Brinchang

Kampong Orang Asli

6

Sam Poh Buddhist Temple

Bukit Perdah ▲

12

■ All Souls' – 3 –

7

○ Kampong Taman Sedia

2

10

Gunung Jasar (1696 m) ▲

11

5

3

Gunung Beremban (1840 m) ▲

4 *Parit Falls*

Tanah Rata

Mardi Agricultural Station

7

Bukit Mentigi ▲

8

Robinson Falls

Bharat Tea Estate

9

Robinson Falls Power Station

9a

Boh Tea Estate

Habu Power Station

Horse Spelling Station

Youland Flower Nursery

Bharat Tea Estate

Gunung Emas (Gold Dollar) Tea Estate

Ringlet Lake

5

Ringlet

Sultan Abu Bakar Dam

PAHANG

PERAK

Numbers refer to trails, see box overleaf

N

1 km
1 mile

To Tapah ►

Where to stay 🛏
Equatorial Hill Resort **4**
Lakehouse **5**

Merlin **6**
Smokehouse **7**
Strawberry Park Resort **8**

strawberry, rose and bee farms. **Tourism Pahang**, www.pahangtourism.com.my, publishes a free guide. Also see www.cameronhighlands.com.

Ringlet

Ringlet, the first township on the road to the Cameron Highlands is not the most attractive place, with 1960s apartment blocks, a cluster of hawker stalls in the town centre and a well-used temple. The main reason for coming here is to visit the **BOH (Best of Highlands) tea plantations** ① *8 km northeast of town, www.boh.com.my, free guided tours every hour*, where you can see the tea being picked and packed. After Ringlet, the road follows a wide river to a lake, connected to a hydroelectric dam. From here a road leads up to the plantation.

Tanah Rata

Tanah Rata is the biggest of the three Cameronian towns and is a good base for walking. It is a friendly place, with a resort atmosphere rather like an English seaside town. There are souvenir shops selling Asli crafts, ranging from blowpipes to woodcarvings. **Gan Seow Hooi**, seowhooigan@hotmail.com, will let customers sample the local high-grade leaf tea. It is worth a visit for the traditional tea ceremony as well as the tea itself. The shop also stocks traditional Chinese clay teapots and other handicrafts.

Brinchang and around

In recent years Brinchang, 7 km beyond Tanah Rata, on the far side of the golf course, has grown fast and new hotels have sprung up, mainly catering for Malaysian Chinese and Singaporean package tourists. The **Sam Poh Buddhist Temple**, perched high on a hill just outside Brinchang, is a colourful sight, with its monumental double gates and dragons. The inner chamber with its six red-tiled pillars holds a vast golden effigy of a Buddha.

From the market area in town, the first road on the right leads to **Kea Farm** ① *www.keafarm.com*, with its neatly terraced hillsides. From here, fruit and vegetables associated with more temperate climates, such as cabbages, cauliflowers, carrots, tomatoes, strawberries and passion fruit, are taken by truck to the supermarkets of KL and Singapore. There is a farm shop and restaurant at the turning on the main road.

The **Rose Garden** is 2 km further up the mountain. To get there, take the first left turn after the butterfly farm, on Jalan Gunung Brinchang, a very picturesque narrow road. A few kilometres further on is a turning for the **Sungai Palas Tea Plantation** ① *www.boh.com.my, Tue-Sun 0900-1630, free guided tours*. The visitor centre has a video about tea cultivation and a shop, as well as a charming terrace where you can enjoy tea and scones and dramatic views across the steeply terraced tea plantations.

From the junction with Jalan Gunung Brinchang, a road continues 13 km into the mountains to the **Blue Valley Tea Estate**. At the village of Trinkap, a right turn leads to a large rose-growing area, **Rose Valley** ① *daily 0800-1800, RM3*, which boasts 450 varieties of rose including the thornless rose, the green rose and the elusive black rose.

Ipoh and around → *For listings, see pages 48-62.*

Malaysia's third city, Ipoh, is situated in the Kinta Valley which is famous for its tin ore production. Few tourists spend long here; most are en route to Penang, KL or Pulau Pangkor. Those who do stay rarely regret it: there are excellent Chinese restaurants (a speciality is the rice noodle dish, *sar hor fun*, which literally means 'melts in your mouth'), Buddhist temples and examples of Straits Chinese architecture. There are also some fine colonial buildings housing notable sights such as the Perak Darul Ridzuan Museum, which provides an interesting insight into Ipoh's history. The city is surrounded by imposing limestone outcrops. These jungle-topped hills, with their precipitous white cliffs, are riddled with passages and caves, many of which have been made into temples. Within easy reach of the city is the Sam Poh Tong, the largest cave temple in the area, and Perak Tong, one of the largest Chinese temples in Malaysia.

Close to Ipoh are the royal town of Kuala Kangsar, the ancient town of Taiping with its strong Chinatown, Lumut, a holiday destination on the coast, and the pleasant island of Pulau Pangkor with good beaches and coral.

Arriving in Ipoh
Getting there and around Ipoh is around 200 km north of KL. The airport is 15 km south of town; at the time of writing, the only connections were with Singapore. From the train station on the edge of town there are connections with Butterworth and KL as well as south to Singapore and north to Hat Yai in Thailand. Ipoh is on the main north–south highway and there are regular connections with anywhere of any size on the Peninsula. The long-distance bus terminal is several kilometres north of town and requires a taxi or bus ride to reach. Shared taxis run to KL, Butterworth, Taiping, Alor Star and Tapah. The grid layout of the town's streets makes it easy to navigate.

Tourist information There are three tourist offices, none of which is particularly helpful: **Ipoh City Council Tourist Office** ⓘ *Jln Abdul Adil, Mon-Thu 0800-1245, 1400-1615, Fri 0800-1230, 1400-1615, Sat 0800-1245;* **Perak Information Centre** ⓘ *Pejabat Setiausaha Kerajaan, Lot 7, Jln Medan Istana 3, T05-255 2772, www.peraktourism.com, Mon-Thu 0800-1245, 1400-1615, Fri 0800-1215, 1445-1615, Sat 0800-1245;* **Tourist Information** ⓘ *Casuarina Hotel, 18 Jln Gopeng, T05-253 2008.*

Places in Ipoh
The Kinta River, spanned by the Hugh Low Bridge, separates the old and new parts of town. The **Old Town** is known for its old Chinese and British colonial architecture, particularly on Jalan Sultan Yusuf, Jalan Leech and Jalan Treacher. Prominent landmarks include the **Birch Memorial**, a clocktower erected in memory of the first British resident of Perak, JWW Birch. The four panels decorating the base of the tower depict the development of civilization. The Moorish-style **railway station** (off Jalan Kelab), was built in 1917 and is known as the 'Taj Mahal' of Ipoh. The **Station Hotel** is a colonial classic.

Heading north out of town past **St Michael's School**, on Jalan Panglima Bukit Gantang Wahab, after about 500 m on the right, is an elegant white colonial building housing the **Perak Darul Ridzuan Museum** ⓘ *www.muziumperak.gov.my, Sat-Thu 0930-1700, Fri 0930-1200 and 1445-1700, free.* The building, more than 100 years old, once the home of Malay dignitaries of Kinta, now holds a collection showing the history of Ipoh, and mining and forestry within the state.

Around Ipoh
The Lost World Of Tambun Water Park ⓘ *Sunway City Ipoh (RM12 taxi ride from town), T05-542 8888, www.sunwaylostworldoftambun.com, Mon, Wed, Thu, Fri 1100-1800, Sat-Sun 1000-1800, closed Tue, RM38, children RM32,* is a new theme park based loosely around the concept of a mythical ancient civilisation where rides are built amongst ruins, waterfalls and the sound of growling beasts in the surrounding jungle. Key attractions are the musical body wash, where visitors can splash around in a musical shower, the river and

beach gardens, and the wave pool. There's also Tiger Valley, with daily tiger feedings at 1500 and 1600, as well as some relaxing hot springs for parents to enjoy while the kids are running wild on the waterslides. This park is a worthwhile day trip for those with children It's possible to visit the hot springs at night on Friday and Saturday (1800-2100, RM5).

At Gunung Rapatm, 5 km south of Ipoh is **Sam Poh Tong** ⓘ *0730-1800, take Kampar bus No 66*, the largest of the cave temples in the area, with Buddha statues among the stalactites and stalagmites. The temple was founded 100 years ago by a monk who lived and meditated in the cave for 20 years and it has been inhabited by monks ever since. The only break was during the Japanese occupation when the cave was turned into a Japanese ammunition and fuel dump.

The ornately decorated **Perak Tong** ⓘ *6.5 km north of Ipoh on Jln Kuala Kangsar, 0900-1600, take Kuala Kangsar bus or city bus No 3*, is one of the largest Chinese temples in Malaysia. Built in 1926 by a Buddhist priest from China, the temple houses more than 40 Buddha statues and traditional Chinese-style murals depicting legends. It is visited by thousands of pilgrims every year. A path beyond the altar leads into the cave's interior and up a brick stairway to an opening 100 m above ground with a view of the surrounding countryside. Another climb leads to a painting of Kuan Yin, Goddess of Mercy, who looks out from the face of the limestone cliff. A 15-m-high reinforced concrete statue of the Buddha stands in the compound.

A 30-minute drive south of Ipoh, **Kellie's Castle** ⓘ *daily 0900-1800, RM4 (child RM3)*, is the eccentric edifice of Scotsman William Kellie Smith, a late 19th-century rubber tycoon. The fanciful Moorish-style mansion was never completed as Smith died during its construction (rumour has it, after inhaling the smoke of a poisoned cigar). During the Second World War the grounds were used by the Japanese as an execution area; locals say it is haunted.

Kuala Kangsar

Halfway between Ipoh and Taiping is the royal riverside town Kuala Kangsar. It is a pleasant place to stop off, with plenty of atmosphere. The first monument you come to is the **Ubudiah Mosque** (1917), one of the most beautiful mosques in the country with its golden domes and elegant minarets. Overlooking the mosque is the residence of the Perak royal family, **Istana Iskandariah** (1930). It is a massive marble structure with a series of towers, topped by golden onion domes set among trees and rolling lawns. The former yellow palace, **Istana Kenangan**, is open to the public and houses the **Museum di Raja (Perak Royal Museum)** ⓘ *T05-776 5500, Sat-Wed 0900-1700 Thu 0900-1245, free*, which exhibits royal regalia. It is a fine example of Malay architecture. Kuala Kangsar is famed for being the site where Malaysia's first rubber trees were grown; the last remaining tree is marked with a plaque. Across the road is the attractive red-roofed building of the **Malay College**, where novelist Anthony Burgess once worked. Considered the Eton of Malaysia, the school was built in 1905 for the children of the royal family.

Taiping

With a backdrop of the Bintang Mountains, Taiping is one of the oldest towns in Malaysia. Around 1840, Chinese immigrants started mining tin in the area and it is the only big Malaysian town with a Chinese name. The town is busy and friendly, with a close-knit, community atmosphere. There is more colonial-era architecture here than in many of Malaysia's towns; there are some fine examples on Jalan Kota, Jalan Main and Jalan Station.

In 1890 the **Lake Garden** was set up on the site of an abandoned tin mine. It is very lush due to the high rainfall and is the pride of the town. Covering 66 ha, the park lies at the foot of **Bukit Larut (Maxwell Hill)**, and has a zoo at its southern end. Built in 1883, the lovely colonial **Perak Museum** ① *Jln Taming Sari (Main Rd), opposite the prison, Sun-Thu 0900-1700, Fri 0900-1200, 1430-1730, free,* is the oldest in Malaysia, dating from 1883. It contains ancient weapons, aboriginal implements, stuffed animals and archaeological finds.

Maxwell Hill ① *T05-806 6789, daily 0800-1700,* is just 12 km or so east of the Lake Garden. Most people climb the hill, whether on foot or by Land Rover (RM7 to summit).

Lumut

Lumut is primarily a base for the Royal Malaysian Navy and is also a transit point for Pulau Pangkor. There is a **tourist office** ① *Jln Sultan Idris Shah, opposite the jetty, T05-683 4057, Mon-Fri 0900-1700, Sat 0900-1345.* The town is at its zenith during the **Pesta Laut**, a sea festival, which takes place every August at nearby the popular beach spot of **Teluk Batik**, 7 km south (taxi from Lumut RM25).

Pulau Pangkor

① *Regular half-hour departures by boat from Lumut (RM10). Taxis and minibuses provide transport on the island. It's also possible to hire motorbikes and bicycles.*

Just 7 km across the Straits from Lumut is Pangkor, one of the most easily accessible islands in Malaysia. Once used as a leper colony, the island was settled by Chinese families in the 1950s, who built a vibrant cottage industry producing dried and salted fish. Now, it's home to some laid-back resorts and great seafood restaurants as well, which are virtually deserted during the week but packed with holidaying locals at weekends. While some of the beaches are a bit grubby, it's possible to hire a motorbike and laze on some fine secluded sands. The island is small enough to walk round in one day and the interior consists of pristine jungle.

In the south of the island are ruins of a Dutch fort, **Kota Belanda**, built by the Dutch East India Company in 1680 to protect the rich tin traders from Malay pirates. **Pangkor village** is also attractive; its main street lined with stores selling dried fish. Some of the coffee houses along the street still have their original marble-topped tables and Straits wooden chairs.

Pulau Penang → *For listings, see pages 48-62.*

Penang – or, more properly, Pulau Pinang – is the northern gateway to Malaysia and is the country's oldest British settlement. It has been sold to generations of tourists as 'the Pearl of the Orient', but in shape Penang looks more like a frog than a pearl. Although the island is best known as a beach resort, it is also a cultural melting pot with Chinese, Malay and Indian influences. Georgetown has the largest collection of pre-war houses in all Southeast Asia.

Penang has managed to preserve at least some of its heritage while that in other Malaysian towns has been torn down partly because of a rent control act – on the statute books for years – which has frozen rents and therefore made redevelopment unprofitable. While the houses may be mouldering, at least they aren't (usually) being demolished. This, however, may all change, as this rent control has now been lifted. In July 2008, Penang was awarded UNSECO World Heritage status along with Melaka. However, not all of the island is worthy of such a status. Pollution and litter have spoiled parts of Penang in recent years. Some beaches are dirty and very few people swim in the sea. The coral that used to line the shore at Batu Feringghi has all gone, mainly due to the silt washed around the headland during the construction of the Penang Bridge. But the sea is not as dirty as in some of the region's other big resorts, as testified by the presence of otters on the beach at Batu Feringghi in the early morning.

In Malay, *pinang* is the word for the areca nut palm, an essential ingredient of bete[
nut. The palm was incorporated into the state crest in the days of the Straits Settlements
during the 19th century. Today Pulau Pinang is translated as 'betel-nut island'.

Visiting Pulau Penang
Getting there Penang International Airport, T04-643 4411, is 20 km south of Georgetown
and receives flights from KL, Johor Bahru and Langkawi as well international destinations.
Taxis to town operate on a coupon system (30 minutes, RM38). **Rapid Penang** bus U401E

① Penang

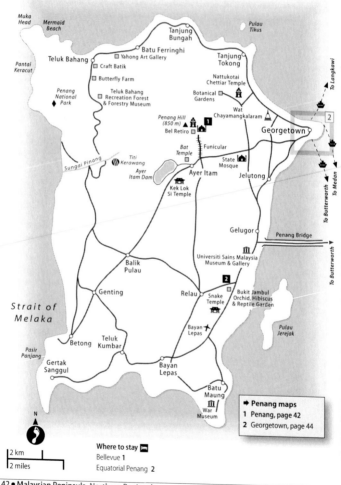

Where to stay 🛏
Bellevue 1
Equatorial Penang 2

The first British settlement

In the late 18th century, Penang was ruled by the Sultan of Kedah and suffered repeated invasions by the Thais from the north and Bugis pirates from the sea. When Captain Francis Light arrived in 1786, aboard a ship of a British trading company, he was looking for a trading base on the north shore of the Strait of Melaka. Light struck a deal with the sultan: he promised to provide military protection in exchange for using Penang as a port. A township grew up around the camp by the harbour and soon became the first British settlement on the Malay Peninsula.

Light declared Penang a free port and Georgetown became the capital of the newly established Straits Settlements. But the glory was short-lived. Following Raffles' founding of Singapore in 1819, Georgetown was quickly eclipsed by the upstart at the southern tip of the Peninsula and by the 1830s had been reduced to a colonial backwater. From an architectural perspective, this proved a saving grace; unlike Singapore, Penang suffered little damage in the Second World War and retains many of its original colonial buildings and rich cultural heritage.

runs from the airport every half hour 0635-2300, RM2, stopping at KOMTAR and Pengkalan Weld and Pengkalan Weld. The island is linked with the mainland via the 13-km Penang Bridge (one-way toll to the mainland RM7). There are direct bus links with KL and a host of Peninsula towns, as well as services to Thailand and Singapore. Trains run as far as Butterworth (see page 47) from where ferries make regular crossings, or local taxis make the run across the bridge to the island. Georgetown also has ferry links with Langkawi and from there on to Thailand. ▸▸ *See Transport, page 59.*

Getting around A free shuttle runs a circuit of 19 tourist destinations in Georgetown every 15 minutes 0600-2400; stops are marked with red circular signs enclosing a number. There are plenty of city buses and taxis in town. It is possible to hire cars, motorbikes and bicycles to explore the island. Bicycle rickshaws carry two people and are one of the most practical ways to explore Georgetown.

Orientation The capital, **Georgetown**, is on the northeast point of the island, nearest the mainland. The 13-km Penang Bridge, linking the island to Butterworth, is halfway down the east coast. **Batu Ferringhi**, on the north coast, is Penang's most famous beach with a strip of luxury hotels. There are secluded coves with good beaches on the northwest tip of the island. The west is a mixture of jungle-covered hills, rubber plantations and a few fishing kampongs. There are more beaches and fishing villages on the south coast. A short, steep mountain range forms a central spine, including **Penang Hill**, at 850 m above sea level. Street names in Georgetown are known by both their Malay and English names.

Tourist information Penang Tourist Centre ⓘ *Penang Port Commission Building, opposite Fort Cornwallis, T04-262 0202, www.tourismpenang.com.my, Mon-Fri 0900-1800, Sat 0800-1300, closed 1st and 3rd Sat;* Tourism Malaysia Northern Regional Office ⓘ *10 Jln Tun Syed Sheh Barakbah, T04-262 0066.* One of the best places is the **Tourist Information Centre** ⓘ *KOMTAR Tower, Jln Penang, T04-261 4461; also at Batu Ferringhi, and the airport, T04-643 0501, Mon-Sat 1000-1800.*

Georgetown

Georgetown is one of Malaysia's most appealing cities and has largely retained its rich cultural heritage. These days, the population is predominantly Chinese and the streets are atmospheric with rickshaws, shophouses, temples and colonial buildings. It's a popular stop for backpackers, with plenty of budget accommodation, cheap restaurants and lively nightlife, particularly around **Love Lane** (officially called Lorong Cinta). The original four streets of Georgetown – Beach (now known as Lebuh Pantai), Lebuh Light, Jalan Masjid Kapitan Kling (previously Lebuh Pitt) and Lebuh Chulia – still form the main thoroughfares. The town was named after King George IV as it was acquired on his birthday; most Malaysians know the town by its nickname, Tanjung.

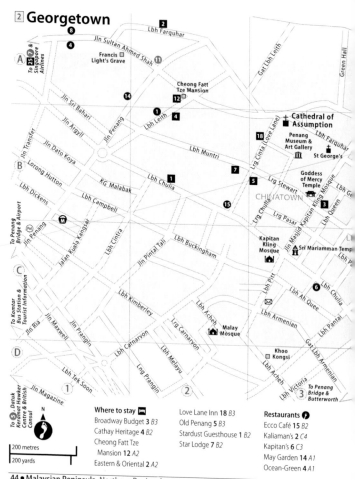

Georgetown

Francis Light's Grave

Cheong Fatt Tze Mansion

Cathedral of Assumption

Penang Museum & Art Gallery

St George's

Goddess of Mercy Temple

CHINATOWN

Kapitan Kling Mosque

Sri Mariamman Temple

Malay Mosque

Khoo Kongsi

To Penang Bridge & Butterworth

Where to stay 🛏

Broadway Budget **3** *B3*
Cathay Heritage **4** *B2*
Cheong Fatt Tze Mansion **12** *A2*
Eastern & Oriental **2** *A2*
Love Lane Inn **18** *B3*
Old Penang **5** *B3*
Stardust Guesthouse **1** *B2*
Star Lodge **7** *B2*

Restaurants 🍴

Ecco Café **15** *B2*
Kaliaman's **2** *C4*
Kapitan's **6** *C3*
May Garden **14** *A1*
Ocean-Green **4** *A1*

On the north tip of the island, **Fort Cornwallis** ⓘ *Tue-Sun 0830-1830, RM3*, marks the site where the British fleet, under Captain Francis Light, first arrived on 16 July 1786. Only its outer walls remain but the amphitheatre hosts concerts and shows. Just opposite the fort, the **Penang Clocktower** was built to commemorate Queen Victoria's Diamond Jubilee. The tower is 60-ft high: one foot for each year of her reign. **Lebuh Pantai** has several interesting buildings including the **ABN-AMRO Arts Centre** ⓘ *No 9, Mon-Sat 0900-1700, free*. It has a stage for *gamelan* recitals and an art gallery with great photo exhibitions. Recommended.

In the heart of Chinatown, near the cathedral, the **Penang Museum and Art Gallery** ⓘ *corner of Lebuh Light and Lebuh Farquhar, T04-263 1942, Sat-Thu 0900-1700, RM1*, has a fine collection of photographs, maps and historical records charting the growth of Penang from the days of Francis Light. Next to the museum, **St George's Church** ⓘ *Lebuh Farquhar*, was the first Anglican church in Southeast Asia, designed by Captain Robert Smith and built by convict labour in 1817.

The **Goddess of Mercy Temple (Kuan Yin Teng)** ⓘ *Jln Kapitan Kling Mosque/Lorong Steward*, was built at in the 1800s by early Chinese immigrants. Kuan Yin is associated with peace, fortune and fertility. Shops sell lanterns, provisions for the afterlife (such as paper Mercedes cars), incense and figurines.

Georgetown also has significant Indian and Muslim populations. The Hindu **Sri Mahamariamman Temple**, on Lebuh Queen/Lebuh Chulia, dates to 1883 and is intricately decorated with deities and mythical animals. The surrounding area is packed with money changers, jewellery shops, tea stalls and banana-leaf restaurants. the Indo-Moorish **Kapitan Kling Mosque** was built by the first Indian Muslim settlers around 1800.

Heading south, on Jalan Acheh the lavishly decorated **Khoo Kongsi** ⓘ *T04-261 2119, Mon-Fri 0900-1700, Sat 0900-1300, RM5*, is one of the most interesting sights in Georgetown. A *kongsi* is a Chinese clan house, which doubles as a temple and a meeting place. It contains some fine art and sculpture.

West of the cathedral, **Cheong Fatt Tze Mansion** ⓘ *14 Lebuh Leith, T04-262 0006, www.cheongfattttzemansion.com, RM12*, is the Chinese equivalent of a stately home and one of only three surviving mansions in this style; the others are in Manila and Medan

➡ **Penang maps**
1 Penang, page 42
2 Georgetown, page 44

Jln Tun Syed Sheh Barakbah

Jln Padang Kota Lama

Jln Tun Syed Sheh Barakbah

Fort Cornwallis

ⓘ Tourism Malaysia

Penang Tourist Centre

Lbh Union

Immigration

ⓘ Penang Clocktower

Swettenham Pier

Lbh Bishop

Lbh Pantai

ABN-AMRO Arts Centre

Danish Consul

Gat Lbh Gereja

Penang & Long Distance Buses

Weld Quay (Pengkalan Weld)

Jln Pengkalan Weld

Taxis

To Butterworth

Pengkalan Raja Tun Uda

To Medan (Sumatra) & Langkawi Island

Red Garden Night
  Market **1** *B2*
The Sire **3** *B4*
Thirty Two **8** *A1*

Bars & clubs ♻
Chillout Club **7** *A1*
Garage **11** *A2*
George's at Sunway
  Hotel **5** *D1*

(Sumatra). It is possible to stay in one of the 16 decadent bedrooms. Parts of the film *Indochine* were shot here.

Around the island

From Georgetown, the round-island trip is a 70-km circuit. It is recommended as a day trip as there is little accommodation outside Georgetown apart from the north coast beaches. It's possible to hire a car or motorbike, or take a tour. ▸▸ *See What to do, page 56.*

The majority of visitors to Penang head straight to **Batu Ferringhi**, the island's main beach. Once a nirvana for Western hippies it has been transformed into an upmarket resort with scores of luxury hotels. Most holidaymakers stick to their hotel swimming pools because the sea is polluted and can be affected by jellyfish. Hotels offer abundant activities, especially watersports. There are also many excellent restaurants, hawker stalls and handicraft shops.

At the western end of the beach is the small fishing kampong of **Teluk Bahang** where the Malabar fishermen used to live. It has been dramatically changed by the **Penang Mutiara Beach Resort**. Beyond Teluk Bahang, around **Muka Head**, the coast is broken into a series of small coves separated by rocky headlands with secluded beaches. Trails lead over the headland from the fishing kampong. One trail goes along the coast past to the **Muka Head lighthouse** (1½ hours); another leads over the headland to **Pantai Keracut** (two hours).

In the centre of the island, a **funicular railway** ① *every 30 mins, 0630-2330*, climbs 850 m up **Penang Hill** ① *bus No 204 to Ayer Itam Station, then shuttle bus No 8 to the railway; most buses from Stand 3 go to Penang Hill*. Completed in 1899, it was Malaysia's first colonial hill station. There are good views from the top, as well as pretty gardens, a temple, mosque and some restaurants. A well-marked 8-km path leads down to the Moon Gate at the **Botanical Gardens** (about an hour's walk) from between the post office and the police station; a steep but delightful descent. The hill supports the last path of tropical rainforest on Penang and is of considerable natural value.

South of Ayer Itam, **Kek Lok Si Temple** ① *0900-1800, free, donation to climb the 30-m tower, bus No 201 and 204, followed by a 5-min walk*, sprawls for 12 ha and can be seen from some distance away. It took Burmese, Chinese and Thai artisans, who were shipped in especially, two decades to build it. The seven-tier pagoda, or **Ban Po**, combines Chinese design with Thai-Buddhist and Burmese, and is covered with thousands of gilded statues.

Other sights of possible interest include the **Snake Temple** ① *12 km south of Georgetown, T04-643 7273, 0600-1900, free, bus No 401*, built in 1850. Snakes were kept in the temple as they were believed to be the disciples of the deity Chor Soo Kong, to whom the temple is dedicated. The number of snakes in the temple varies from day to day – there are usually more around during festivals. The incense smoke keeps them in a drugged stupor, and most of them have had their fangs extracted.

Further up the west side of the island is the **Penang National Park**, formerly the **Pantai Acheh Forest Reserve** ① *entrance is through Telok Bahang at the end of Batu Ferringhi Rd, bus No 101 to Telok Bahang; either walk from here or take a boat from the fishing jetty; longer fare stages cost anything up to RM2; as the island buses are infrequent, check departure times at each place to avoid being stranded*. It has well-marked trails into the jungle and to the bays further round; for example, to Pantai Keracut (one hour). After the Pantai Acheh junction, and on up a twisting, forested section of road, there is a waterfall, called **Titi Kerawang**. It has a pleasant pool that's suitable for swimming and is just off the road (20th milestone). The national park, the world's smallest, contains over 410 species of flora and 143 fauna species including dolphins, otters, hawksbill turtles, snakes and macaques and leaf monkeys. Camping facilities are available – enquire at the Wildlife Office in Teluk

Bahang. To get there take bus U101 from Georgetown which travels all the way to the park entrance at Teluk Bahang village. Visitors must register at the **Wildlife Office** ⓘ *Jln Hassan Abas, T04-881 3530, daily 0800-1800, free*, before entering the park.

Butterworth → *Phone code: 04*

This industrial and harbour town and base for the Royal Australian Air Force was billeted here under the terms of the Five Powers Pact. It is the main port for ferries to Penang and most tourists head straight for the island; Butterworth is not a recommended stopping point but there are a couple of hotels, should you get stuck.

Pulau Langkawi → *For listings, see pages 48-62.*

The Langkawi group is an archipelago of 99 islands around 30 km off the west coast of Peninsula Malaysia. Pulau Langkawi itself, by far the largest of the group, is a mountainous, palm-fringed island with scattered fishing kampongs, paddy fields and sandy coves. It has seen significant development in recent years and is home to some of Malaysia's most upmarket resorts. Other islands are nothing more than deserted limestone outcrops rearing out of the turquoise sea, cloaked in jungle, and ringed by coral.

The main settlement is in the dusty town of Kuah. There are plenty of top-end resorts, while Pantai Cenang and Tengah also have a smattering of cheaper guesthouses. It's a popular place for those wanting to renew their Thai or Malaysian visas.

Note The sea at Pantai Cenang and Pantai Tengah will come as a disappointment to those who have experienced the Thai islands to the north and the beaches on Malaysia's east coast. Unfortunately, plastic and rubbish from tour boats and larger vessels has dirtied the sea, which can be a little murky anyway. It is best to swim at high tide, and give the sea a miss at low tide. **Zackry's** (see page 52) has a weekly tide chart posted at their reception.

Visiting Pulau Langkawi

Getting there and around Langkawi's International airport ⓘ *20 km from Kuah, T04-955 1311*, has connections with KL, Singapore and Penang. Ferries from Kuala Perlis, the jumping-off point for Pulau Langkawi and Phuket (in Thailand), leave roughly every hour to Langkawi and there are two daily departures from Penang by sea. There are also three daily ferries to Satun (Thailand). Taxis run throughout the island (prices are fixed according to distance). Cars, motorcycles and bicycles are available for hire. Boats are also available to explore the neighbouring islands. ►► *See Transport, page 61.*

Tourist information Langkawi Tourist Information Centre ⓘ *Jln Pesiaran Putra, Kuah, T04-966 7789, daily 0900-1700*. The magazine, *Senses of Langkawi*, has ideas of things to do and where to eat. Also useful are www.langkawi-online.com and www.best-of-langkawi.com.

Places in Pulau Langkawi

The main town, **Kuah**, is strung out along the seafront and is the landing point for ferries from Satun (Thailand), Kuala Perlis, Kuala Kedah and Penang. The jetty is 2 km from Kuah itself. The town is growing fast and developers have reclaimed land along the shoreline to cope with the expansion. The old part of Kuah has several restaurants, a few grotty hotels, banks, plenty of coffee shops and a string of duty-free shops, which do a roaring trade in cheap liquor, cigarettes and electronics. There is also an attractive mosque.

Southwest of Kuah, past beautiful paddy fields and coconut groves, are the two main beaches, Pantai Cenang and Pantai Tengah. **Pantai Cenang** is 2 km long, with a range of accommodation. It's a good place for watersports and home to **Langkawi Underwater World** ① *T04-955 6100, daily 0930-1830 (until 2030 at weekends), RM38, children RM28*, one of Asia's largest aquariums. Just north of Pantai Cenang, the **Muzium Laman Padi (Rice Museum Garden)** ① *T04-955 4312, www.langkawigeopark.com.my, open 1000-1800, free*, explains the stages of rice farming and has a rooftop rice garden and restaurant. There is a 3.5-ha paddy field, where visitors can have a wander and a herb garden and guides offer informative tours describing medicinal uses of the herbs.

Most of the new beach chalet development is along the 3-km stretch of coast from Pantai Cenang to **Pantai Tengah**, at the far southern end around a small promontory. Pantai Tengah is less developed and quieter than Pantai Cenang. **Note** The sea at Pantai Cenang and Pantai Tengah will come as a disappointment to those who have experienced the Thai islands to the north or the beaches on Malaysia's east coast. Unfortunately, plastic and rubbish from tour boats and larger vessels has dirtied the sea, which can be a little murky anyway. It is best to swim at high tide, and give the sea a miss at low tide. **Zackry's** guesthouse has a weekly tide chart posted at their reception.

The road west leads past the airport to **Pantai Kok**, on the magnificent **Burau Bay**. Once unspoilt, it is now spotted with upmarket resorts and a fancy marina.

There are several isolated beaches along the bay, accessible by boat from either Pantai Kok itself, Pantai Cenang (12 km away) or Kampong Kuala Teriang, a fishing village en route. On the west headland, the **Telaga Tujuh waterfalls** are not as impressive as they used to be thanks to a pipeline running next to them to Berjaya Langkawi Beach Resort.

Northern Peninsula listings

For hotel and restaurant price codes and other relevant information, see pages 9-11.

⊖ Where to stay

Cameron Highlands *p36, map p37*
There are some excellent mid-range and budget choices here, with hotels and guesthouses usually offering tour and ticketing services. Touts will meet new arrivals at the bus station and offer them a lift back to the hotel of their choice. More popular places get booked out well in advance Book in advance for public or school holidays (Apr, Aug, Dec). Prices rise by 30-50% at this time. The cheapest option if in a group is to share a bungalow. Most bungalows have gardens, log fires and are out of town.

Ringlet *p38*
$$$ Lakehouse, T05-495 6152, www. lakehouse-cameron.com. This is located a few kilometres outside of Ringlet but has fantastic lake views. It is a Tudor-style country house, the final brainchild of Colonel Stanley Foster, with 18 rooms of antique furnishings, 4-poster beds and en suite bathrooms, overlooking the lake. The restaurant serves English food and the **Cameron Bar** and **Highlander Lounge** both have an English country pub atmosphere. A great place to stay and reasonable value.

Tanah Rata *p38*
$$$$ Smokehouse, T05-491 1215, www.thesmokehouse.com.my/ch.htm. This place is modelled on its namesake, the Smokehouse in Mildenhall (UK) and it preserves its home counties ethos and 'ye olde English' style of old-time resident Colonel Stanley Foster. Its rooms are

first class, there is an original red British telephone box in the garden and the restaurant serves expensive English food.

$$-$ Father's Guest House, Jln Gereja, T05-491 2484, www.fathers.cameron highlands.com. Near the convent, up a long flight of steps (look for the sign with Bob Marley). This former seminary is the best budget bet in town and consistently full. It has a very friendly atmosphere and a great communal area with beautiful views. It occupies the entire hill and has plenty of lawn and a small lounge for evening beers and cable TV. The dorms and cheaper rooms are located in old Nissan huts. The main building has a good selection of clean, comfy rooms with terrace, some have Wi-Fi access. Tours to the tea plantations and butterfly garden depart daily. The **Secret Garden Café** is a great place for breakfast. There's free pick-up from the bus station and staff can also arrange trips and transfers to other sites and areas. Essential to book in advance. Highly recommended.

$ Cameronian Inn, 16 Jln Mentigi, T05-491 1327, www.thecameronianinn. com. Sparkling floors make this one of the cleanest budget digs in the Highlands, with a selection of simple, but comfortable rooms, most of which have windows. There's an inexpensive café serving toasted sandwiches, TV room, internet, and a decent expanse of lawn with chairs for soaking up the mountain rays. Recommended.

$ Hillview Inn, 17 Jln Mentigi, T05-491 2915, www.hillview-inn.com. Charming house with spacious rooms. Facilities include TV, internet, laundry, book exchange, beautiful garden and restaurant. Very quiet and spotlessly clean. Recommended.

Brinchang and around *p38*
$$ Rainbow, Lot 25, T05-491 4628. Corner hotel with 36 good-value comfortable rooms all with TV and minibar. Good views on one side. Recommended, but no restaurant.

$$-$ Pines and Roses, T05-491 2203. Good-value family rooms or dorms, TV and water heater, basic furnishings, clean.
$ Kowloon, 34-35 Jln Besar, T05-491 1366. Above a popular Chinese restaurant, nice rooms with shower, good value for money.

Ipoh and around *p38*
$$$-$$ Majestic Station, Bangunan Stesen Keretapi, Jln Panglima Bukit Gantang Wahab, T05-255 5605, www. majesticstationhotel.com. On the 3rd floor of the railway station, this hotel offers an excellent opportunity to stay in a gorgeous colonial building on the cheap. Rooms are a bit gloomy, but large and there is a wonderful terrace with a café overlooking the Ipoh Town Hall. Stay here before developers get their hands on it. Recommended.

$$$-$$ Merloon, 92-98 Jln Mustapha al-Bakri, T05-253 6755. Big, old, airy building with large, clean rooms with attached bath.
$$$-$$ Robin, 106-110 Jln Mustapha al-Bakri, T05-241 3755. Same owner as the **Merloon** and next door, but about RM10 pricier. Rambling, empty corridors and spacious, clean a/c rooms with TV and fridge. What this hotel lacks in ambience, it makes up for in location and price. Recommended.

$$ Fair Park, 85 Jln Kamaruddin Isa, T05-548 8666, www.fairparkhotel.com. One of the newer budget hotels, near DBI Sports Centre and with a selection of clean a/c rooms with Wi-Fi, cable TV and attached bathroom. This is one of the best value places to stay in Ipoh, but is located 25 mins' walk from the city centre. Recommended.

$$ New Caspian, 6 Jln Jubilee Pitchay, T05-242 3327. This garish blue and purple building has a selection of clean and comfortable rooms offering reasonable value for money with TV, fridge and a/c. A good location with lots of late-night cafés and Chinese restaurants.

Kuala Kangsar *p40*

$$ Rest House (Rumah Rehat Kuala Kangsar), Bukit Candan, T05-776 5872. Pleasant location inside the gates to the palace road. Old colonial mansion with huge a/c rooms, with bathroom and hot water, some rooms face the river. Friendly, helpful.

$ Double Lion, 74 Jln Kasa, 300 m from the bus station, T05-776 8010. Some a/c, pleasant enough, large rooms, some overlook the river.

Taiping *p40*

$$ Legend Inn, 2 Jln Long Jaafar, T05-806 0000, www.legendinn.com. Hotel block with 88 rooms, bath, TV, video channel, coffee house, plushest place in town, well-equipped.

$ New Champagne, 17 Jln Lim Sweeaqun, T05-806 5060, www.newchampagnehotel. com. Opposite Cathay Cinema. Friendly, helpful staff, pleasant and clean.

$ Rumah Rehat Baru, 1 Jln Sultan Mansor, Taman Tasek, T05-807 2044. Restaurant, a little out of town, the new block is hardly attractive but rooms are large with en suite, overlooks the Lake Garden and is good value.

Lumut *p41*

$$ Lumut Country Resort, 331 Jln Titi Panjang, T05-683 5109, www.lumutcountry resort.biz. Offers 44 a/c rooms, swimming pool, tennis courts, hand-printed batik bed covers and wooden floors. Disco, function room. One of the best deals in town.

$ Harbour View, Lot 13 and 14, Jln Titi Panjang, T05-683 7888. Small, quiet hotel on main road along seafront, a/c, TV, fridge, bathroom. Good value.

Pulau Pangkor *p41*

Hotels offer discounts during the week but increase 50% during holidays. Many budget places are at Teluk Nipah on the west coast.

$$$$ Pangkor Laut Resort, T800 9899 9999, www.pangkorlautresort.com. One of Malaysia's top resort. Idyllic with magnificently set chalets over the sea

(linked by wooden walkways) or on the jungled hillside. Wildlife is abundant and the jungle treks are excellent. Highly recommended if you can afford it.

$$ Coral View Beach Resort, Pasir Bogak, T05-685 2190. Cute chalets on hillside surrounded by trees; very tranquil. Restaurant, good views, motorbike hire.

$ Joe Fisherman Village, Teluk Nipah, T05-685 2389. Popular budget place with A-frame chalets and 2 mattresses on the floor, bicycles for hire, meals available.

$ Vikry Resort, Pasir Bogak, T05-685 4258. Offers 10 a/c chalets in spacious grounds. The Indian restaurant is excellent. Friendly staff.

Georgetown *p44, map p44*

Most upmarket hotels are around Jln Penang. Cheaper hotels are on Lebuh Chulia and Lebuh Leith.

$$$$ Eastern & Oriental (**E&O**), 10 Lebuh Farquhar, T04-222 2000, www.e-o-hotel. com. A/c, restaurant, pool, built in 1885 by the Armenian Sarkies brothers, who operated Singapore's **Raffles Hotel** and the **Strand Hotel** in Rangoon (Yangon). Noël Coward and Somerset Maugham figured on former guest lists. This stunning hotel has been restored to its former glory. Staff are friendly and efficient, atmosphere is luxurious. There are fair options for varied cuisine, both international fine dining and local, from coffee houses to ballrooms. Shop, business centre, pool and gym. Excellent promotional rates available – check website

$$$$-$$$ Cheong Fatt Tze Mansion, 14 Leith St, T04-262 0006, www.cheongfatt tzemansion.com. Fully restored 19th-century mansion with elegant themed rooms and period furniture.

$$$-$$ Cathay Heritage, 15 Lebuh Leith, T04-262 6271, cathayhbh@gmail.com. Huge fan and a/c rooms in a detached colonial mansion filled with 1920s furniture including a gorgeous art deco staircase. Fittings are somewhat ancient giving the place a rustic, well-used feel but this hotel s packed with roguish charm.

$$ Star Lodge, 39 Lebuh Muntri, T04-262 6378, www.starlodge.net Owned by the same people at the **75 Travellers Lodge**, this is a slightly more upmarket option with new rooms with windows and attached bath and Wi-Fi. Slightly haphazard when it comes to reservations – confirm your room the day before arrival.

$$-$ Broadway Budget Hotel, 35F Jln Masjid Kapitan Kling, T04-262 8550, www.broadwaybudgethotel.com. Not wildly atmospheric but has 18 comfy, spotless a/c and fan rooms in the heart of town. Free Wi-Fi. Recommended.

$$-$ Love Lane Inn, 54 Love Lane, T016-419 8409, ocean008@hotmail.com. Backpackers' favourite with a wide variety of simple, clean rooms in a rambling 3-storey building. Some rooms have no window. Dorm available (RM12). Shared cold-water bathroom.

$$-$ Old Penang, 53 Lorong Cinta, T04-263 8805, www.oldpenang.com. Clean budget lodgings in a former restaurant, high ceilings and smallish but comfortable rooms with Wi-Fi and a/c or fan. Some rooms are without window. Dorm available (RM10). Recommended

$$-$ Stardust Guesthouse, 370-D Lebuh Chulia, T04-263 5723, www.stardustguest house.com. Simple, clean lodgings located above a busy and at times noisy café. Mixture of fan and a/c rooms with shared bath and free Wi-Fi access. Popular.

Batu Ferringhi

Budget options are clustered by the sea next to the turn-off by the **Grand Plaza Parkroyal**.

$$$$ Rasa Sayang, T04-888 8888, www.shangri-la.com. A/c, restaurants, pool. Probably the most popular on the beach strip, Minangkabau-style, horse-shoe design around a pool and garden. Sophisticated and welcoming.

$ Ah Beng, 54c Batu Ferringhi, right on the beach, T04-881 1036. A/c, clean, rooms with a/c, fan. Friendly, family-run.

$ Baba's, 52 Batu Ferringhi, T04-881 1686, babaguesthouse2000@yahoo.com. Clean, homely and relaxed. Good information. Also owns **ET Budget Guest House**, www. geocities.com/etguesthouse, at No 47.

$ Shalini's, 56 Batu Ferringhi, T04-881 1859, ahlooi@pc.jaring.my. Lovely little house with balcony overlooking the sea. Clean and homely.

Butterworth *p47*

Most hotels are 20 mins' walk from the bus terminal, so a taxi ride is advisable.

$$$ Berlin, 4802 Jln Bagan Luar, T04-332 1701. A/c, TV. The best option. Restaurant next door.

Pulau Langkawi *p47*

Due to the lack of public transport on Langkawi, it is a good idea to book a room ahead or at least have a firm idea of where to be dropped by the taxi, as the resort area is very spread out. The more popular budget options are often booked up in advance and visitors turning up without a booking face a fair chance of being turned away. The island is busy Nov-Feb. Hotels in Kuah tend to be poor value – best to head to the beach.

$$$-$$ Asia, 3A-4A Jln Persiaran Putra, Kuah, T04-966 6216. A/c, reasonable place, 15 mins' walk from the jetty, some dorm beds. Clean and quiet.

Pantai Cenang

Plenty of hotels and chalets; some are cramped a little too closely together. Despite the development, it is a picturesque beach.

$$$$ Bon Ton, T04-955 1688, www. bontonresort.com.my. 100-year-old Malay houses with modern facilities. Pool, jacuzzi, fantastic fusion restaurant. Romantic setting. Unbeatable atmosphere. Recommended.

$$$$-$$$ Beach Garden Resort, T04-955 1363, www.beachgardenresort. com. German owned resort with Malay overtones evident in the rattan furnished rooms with their thatched roofs. Each of the 12 rooms is very comfortable, has marble floor tiling and a/c. There's a small pool and beachside restaurant (with Swiss chef), designed to resemble a Bavarian breakfast room (although the Balinese masks on the walls throw this idea into some chaos).

$$ Sweet Inn, Lot 792, off Jln Pantai Cenang, away from the beach, 100 m down a side road and next to the **Gecko Guesthouse**, T012-493 9718, www.sweet inns.net. This is a great new hotel, offering the best value for money in the mid-range bracket. Rooms are set in an orange concrete block and are simple and clean with TV, mini-fridge, attached bathroom and Wi-Fi access. The downside is its distance from the beach. Recommended.

$ Gecko Guesthouse, T019-428 3801. Tucked away up a lane on the other side of the main road to the beach. Well-decorated rooms, albeit simple with wooden floors and attached cold-water showers. Good bar area, super-relaxed atmosphere, movies and all the regular traveller accessories. This place is prime backpacker territory and is often swarming with people. Can get a bit noisy in the evenings as people take advantage of the cheap booze on offer. The monkeys chained up behind the reception are a bit of a turn off.

Pantai Tengah
$$$ Sunset Beach Resort, T04-955 1751, www.sunvillage.com.my. Beautiful setting, romantic chalets with Balinese furniture and frangipani flowers in the gardens. Stunning.
$ Zackry, right at the south end of Pantai Tengah, T04-955 7595, www.zackry guesthouse.langkawinetworks.com. Another spot swarming with backpackers. It only accepts online bookings and for a minimum of 2 nights. Rooms are a jumbled assortment of a/c and fan, some with attached bathroom. Runs on a trust system, with payment for beers and internet paid by guests at the end of their stay. Great communal bar area, and a communal

kitchen where travellers cook up a storm each evening. It's across the road from the beach. Free bicycle rental. Recommended.

Pantai Kok and Burau Bay
$$$$ Berjaya Langkawi Beach Resort, Burau Bay, T04-959 1888, www.berjaya resorts.com.my. Malaysian-style chalets in tropical rainforest, some on stilts over water, some on jungled hillside. Very comfortably furnished with classical furniture. Excellent facilities, white-sand beach, beach restaurant.
$$$ Mutiara Burau Bay, Jln Teluk Burau, T04-959 1061, www.mutiarahotels.com. A/c, restaurant, at the far end of Pantai Kok. A fun hotel, good for families with a swimming pool and forest or beach horse riding. Excellent café.

❼ Restaurants

Ringlet p36
$$$ Lakehouse. Traditional English food, typical Sun lunch fare and cream teas.

Tanah Rata p38
$$$ Smokehouse. Favourites include beef Wellington, roast beef, Yorkshire pudding, steak and kidney pie and cream teas.
$$ Suria, 66A Jln Perisan Camellia 3. Open 24 hrs. Excellent South Indian food served on a banana leaf, vegetarian options, friendly.
$ Di Chennai, Jln Besar. Superb RM7 delicious tandoori chicken set meals and a host of other veg and non-veg Indian food.
$ T Café, 1F, 4 Jln Besar, T019-5722 8833. Cosy travellers' café with Chinese and Malay dishes as well as Western snacks and cakes, scones and pies. Very friendly and good atmosphere.

Brinchang and around p38
$$ Ferns, Rosa Passadena Hotel. Western and oriental, good-value buffet.
$$ Parkland, Parkland Hotel. Grill restaurant with steaks, breakfast menu.

$ Brinchang, below hotel of the same name on Jln Besar. Popular for its steamboat, good selection of vegetable dishes.
$ Kowloon, Jln Besar. Busy restaurant, lemon chicken and steamboat are popular.

Ipoh and around *p38*

Ipoh is known for its Chinese food, especially Ipoh chicken rice and *kway teow*. The pomelo and the seedless guava are grown in Perak, and the state is known for its groundnuts.
$$$ Royal Casuarina Coffee House, and **Il Ritrove**, 18 Jln Gopeng. Italian restaurant specializing in nouvelle cuisine.
$$ Sushi King and **Restoran MP**, G/F Ipoh Parade. Both have sushi on a conveyer belt and are spotless but somewhat lacking in atmosphere. MP offers hearty steamboats, appropriate in the cool climes of the mall.
$ Benzas, Jln Tun Sambantham. Lovely setting with outdoor seating facing the Padang. This restaurant serves up great North Indian fare. Recommended.
$ Hainam, Jln Mustapha Al-Bakri. Good for a plate of authentic Hainan chicken rice.
$ Idamanan Kopitiam, 27-29 Jln Tun Sambantham. Cosy coffee shop with a superb *penang laksa*. Also, desserts and sandwiches.
$ Kopitian Junction, G/F Ipoh Parade Mall. Popular eatery with a selction of Malay snacks and cooling desserts and drinks such as the delicious mango ice, cucumber and lemon juice. There is even a very local take on sausage and mash.
$ Mee Rebus Ramli, Jln Raja Ezram. Excellent selction of Malay dishes with an emphasis on noodles such as *mee jawa* and *mee rebus* but also a fair choice of rice dishes.

Kuala Kangsar *p40*

Many restaurants only open at lunchtime. The smartest restaurant is at the **Hotel Seri Kangsar**. In front of here is an Indian restaurant open until late. The market has foodstalls and there's a bakery beside the **Double Lion Hotel**.

Taiping *p40*
$$ Nagaria Steak House, 61 Jln Pasar. Dark interior, popular for beer drinking.
$ Kedai Kopi Sentosa, Jln Kelab Cina. Good Teow Chiew noodles.
$ Kum Loong, 45-47 Jln Kota. Good dim sum. Great place to experience local bustle.

Lumut *p41*
$$ Ocean Seafood, 115 Jln Tit Panjang. A/c, specializes in Chinese and seafood.
$ Kedai Makan Sin Pinamhui (Green House), 95 Jln Titi Panjang. Closed Tue. Good Malay.
$ Nasi Kandar, 46 Jln Sultan Idris Shah. Friendly and clean, excellent vegetarian rice and *roti*.

Pulau Pangkor *p41*
Most hotels and chalets have their own restaurants. Seafood is always on the menu
$$$ Pangkor Laut Resort, T05-699 1100, reservations T03-2145 9000, www.pangkor lautresort.com. 3 top-quality restaurants serving seafood, steamboats or Western fare.
$$ Coco, Pasir Bogak. Outdoor seafood restaurant and local dishes.
$ Vikry Resort. Excellent home-cooked Indian dishes on banana leaves.

Georgetown *p44, map p44*
Specialities include *assam laksa* (a hot-and-sour fish soup), *nasi kandar* (curry), *mee yoke* (prawns in chilli-noodle soup) and *inche kabin* (chicken marinated in spices and fried). Penang is known for Nyonya cuisine (see page 10).
$$$ Ocean-Green, 48F Jln Sultan Ahmad Shah (in quiet alleyway in front of **Paramount Hotel**). Specialities include lobster and crab thermidor, drunken prawns and fresh frogs' legs ('paddy chicken'), lovely location, overlooking fishing boats. Recommended.
$$$-$$ Thirty Two, 32 Jln Sultan Ahmad Shah, T04-262 2232. Chinese-owned 1920s mansion. Beautifully maintained. Restaurant has a bar/lounge with live jazz, and a

terrace by the water. Asian fusion cuisine. Friendly and sophisticated.

$$ Ecco Café, 400 Lebuh Chulia. Opens after 1800. Atmospheric bar/Italian café crammed with bizarre objects and Indian tapestries. Very relaxed and friendly hangout. The owner makes his own pizza dough and pasta, to create some of Penang's best Italian food for a reasonable price. Freshly ground coffee, pastas, sandwiches and pizzas including the unconventional banana pizza.

$$ The Sire Museum Restaurant, 4 King St, T04-264 5088. Closed Sun. Attractive restaurant covered in Asian artwork and with a menu offering tasty dishes such as baked portobello mushrooms, crab cakes and a selection of pasta dishes and sandwiches. Excellent choice of beers. Recommended.

$ Kaliaman's, 43 Lebuh Penang. One of Penang's best Indian restaurants with an atmosphere that transports the diner to the streets of Chennai. Excellent South Indian set lunches and a good selection of North Indian à la carte dishes all day. The menu includes favourites such as *roghan josh*, *dopiaza* and spicy *chettinad* curries. Recommended.

$ Kapitan, 93 Lebuh Chulia (near Sri Mahamariamman Temple), T04-264 1191. Patrons flock to this restaurant for a taste of their Indian Muslim cuisine and fabulous tandoori sets and claypot biryanis. Recommended.

$ May Garden, 70 Penang Rd (next to **Towne House**). Good seafood restaurant with a tank full of fish and shellfish to choose from. The speciality is frogs' legs, with chilli and ginger.

Foodstalls Penang's hawker stalls are famous and particularly atmospheric in the evenings. **Red Garden Night Market** on Lebuh Leith has an excellent tourist-friendly hawker centre that comes alive after dark and offers ice-cold beers, Japanese, Thai and local dishes such as chicken rice, *yong tau foo* and fresh seafood. Gets busy at weekends. Recommended. **Datuk Keramat Hawker Centre**, on the junction of Anson and Perak roads, is one of the venues for the roving night market (check with tourist centre, T04-261 6663); also **Padang Kota Lama/Jln Tun Syed Sheh Barakbah** (Esplanade); and **Pesiaran Gurney Seawall** (Gurney Drive), Malay, Chinese and Indian.

Batu Ferringhi and Teluk Bahang

Most big hotels have excellent restaurants.

$$$ House of Four Seasons, Penang Mutiara Beach Resort, Jln Teluk Bahang. Good old-fashioned opulence with an interesting menu, Cantonese and Szechuan dishes.

$$ The Catch, Jln Teluk Bahang. Malay, Chinese, Thai and international seafood dishes, fish tanks for fresh fish, prawns, crabs, lobster, pleasant setting, one of the best.

$ End of the World, end of Teluk Bahang Beach. Huge quantities of fresh seafood, superb chilli crabs and great value lobster (RM25 each), all in a very pleasant setting on the beach.

$ Hollywood, Tanjung Bungah, Batu Ferringhi. Great views over the beach, serves *inche kabin* chicken stews and a good selection of seafood.

$ Papa Din's Bamboo, 124-B Batu Ferringh (turn left after police station, 200 m up the Kampong Rd). Home-cooked fish curries.

Pulau Langkawi *p47*

Langkawi's speciality is *mee gulong* (fried noodles cooked with shredded prawns, slices of beef, chicken, carrots, cauliflower rolled into a pancake and served with a potato gravy). There is lots of Thai influence. The roadside foodstalls down from the **Langkasuka Hotel** in Padang Matsirat are highly recommended.

Kuah

$$ Sari Village, Kompleks Pasar Lama, T04-966 751. On stilts over the sea, with a vast selection of seafood. Beautifully designed with good views. Pakistani-influenced cuisine. Specialities include vegetable curry and fish tandoori.

$ Mai, 131 Langkawi Mall, T04-966 0255. Stylish Thai and Malay food. Set lunch RM10. Mai-blend fruit shake recommended.

Pantai Cenang

$$$ Putumayo, Lot 1584, Jln Pantai Cenang, T04-955 2233. Lunch and dinner. Sophisticated fusion menu, heavy on seafood, in a stylish and elegant setting. The lobster and scallop dishes are divine, as is the fare on the lengthy wine list. Highly recommended.

$$$-$$ Casa del Mar, and the Beach Garden next door, offer international fare, beautifully prepared. The latter is right on the beach.

$$ Nam, inside the Bon Ton Resort, just north of Pantai Cenang. Beautiful restaurant overlooking a lake serving funky fusion food. Try the rock lobster and baked snapper on mango rice. Highly recommended.

$$ Red Tomato Garden Café, T012-513 6046. Closed Fri. German/Malaysian-run, this is one of the most popular places to eat with its freshly baked bread, double-handed sandwiches, extensive breakfast menu and authentic pastas and pizzas. Travellers who have been on the road too long will love this place. Recommended.

$ OK Boss, next to the entrance of Rumours Guesthouse. Opens for dinner only. Excellent little shack, highly popular with locals for its generous portions, friendly service and, most importantly, superb Melakan *asam pedas* cooking. Recommended.

Pantai Tengah

$$$ Unkaizan, T04-955 4118. Great views from the balcony of this upmarket Japanese joint. Expensive but recommended.

$$ The Lighthouse, T04-955 2586. Open 1130-2230. Minimalist place, inspired by its name, with tables right on the beach. Has varied menus; 1 for lunch and 1 for dinner.

Outrageous desserts, lamb shanks, gnocchi and fresh crunchy salads.

$$ Sunvillage and **Matahari Malay**. Both in exquisite surroundings. Extensive menus of traditionally prepared dishes.

Pantai Kok

$$$ Oriental Pearl, Berjaya Langkawi Beach Resort, Burau Bay. Upmarket but simple Chinese, ocean views, good steamboat.

🎵 Bars and clubs

Tanah Rata *p38*

The Lakehouse and Smokehouse hotel bars are also popular venues for their country pub atmosphere and air of exclusivity.

Strawberry Park Resort. The only disco in town, karaoke and a bar.

Traveller's Bistro, Jln Persiaran Camellia. Bar with outside seating and plenty of 1980s rock. Good place to chat to locals.

Georgetown *p44, map p44*

Most of the big hotels have clubs. Expect to pay cover charges if you are not a guest.

Chillout Club, Gurney Hotel, 18 Persiaran Gurney, T04-370 7000. Good dance club with R&B and House music. Popular.

The Garage, 2 Penang Rd, opposite E&O Hotel, T04-263 6868. Open 1100-0300. There are several bars and clubs inside this restored art deco garage including **Slippery Senoritas**, a tapas and salsa bar with live South American music and performing bar staff. Recommended.

George's, Sunway Hotel, 33 New Lane. Quintessentially English, live music.

There is a selection of small bars along Lebuh Chulia, including **Hong Kong Bar** and **Mona Lisa**, that both attract boozy tourists.

Pulau Langkawi *p47*

Pantai Cenang now has a few standalone bars, but they tend to close by 0100. The main places are **Go Slow Café**, right on the beach and the **Irish Bar**, on Jln Pantai Cenang. Pantai Tengah.

SunKarma, Jln Teluk Baru. Daily 1800-2400. This upmarket chillout bar has a long list of cocktails, fascinating toilet design and indoor and outdoor seating. Just down the road and owned by the same guy is **Sunba**, with a more homely, pub-like atmosphere and music long past its sell-by date.

✪ Festivals

Georgetown *p44, map p44*
Feb/Mar Chap Goh Meh, celebrated on the 15th night of the 1st month of the Chinese lunar calendar; girls throw oranges into the sea for their suitors to catch.
May/Jun Dragon Boat 'Tuen Ng' Festival near Penang Bridge. Teams from around the region and beyond compete. The **Floral Festival** at the Botanic Gardens sees city parades by Malays, Chinese and Indians.
Sep Lantern Festival, a parade with lanterns.
Oct/Nov Deepavali Open House, festivities in Little India.

✪ Shopping

Georgetown *p44, map p44*
The main areas are Jln Penang, Jln Burmah and Lebuh Campbell. There is a moveable night market – ask the tourist office for locations.

Antiques An export licence is required for non-imported goods. Shops are concentrated on Jln Penang. There are also antique shops along Rope Walk (Jln Pintal Tali). Most stock antiques from Thailand, Indonesia, Sabah and Sarawak, as well local bargains. **Oriental Arts Co**, 3f Penang Rd, is well established with a fine collection.
Penang Antique House, 27 Jln Patani, sells Peranakan artefacts – porcelain, rosewood with mother-of-pearl inlay.

Batik Maphilindo Baru, 217 Penang Rd, has an excellent range of batiks and sarongs.

Handicrafts Jln Penang is a good place to start. Also try: **Arts and Culture Information Centre**, T04-264 2273.
See Koon Hoe, 315 Lebuh Chulia, sells Chinese opera masks, jade seals and paper umbrellas. **The Garage**, 2 Penang Rd (opposite E&O Hotel), is a bright orange art deco restored garage with gift and souvenir stalls. **Mah Jong Factory**, Love Lane, sells high-quality Mah Jong sets.

Batu Ferringhi and Teluk Bahang
Handicrafts Craft Batik, opposite the ParkRoyal, sells batik cloth by the metre and as ready-made garments. **Yahong Art Gallery**, 58d Batu Ferringhi Rd, T04-881 1251, has batik paintings by the Teng family, considered the father of Malaysian batik. Free entry, excellent quality.

Pulau Langkawi *p47*
Duty free Although Langkawi enjoys duty-free status there is not much reason to come here for the shopping. Duty-free shops line the main street in Kuah and the jetty.

Handicrafts Many shops in Kuah sell textiles. **Batik Jawa Store**, 58 Pekan Pokok Asam, is the best-stocked. **Flint Stones Handicraft**, Jln Pandak Mayah, has good Asian handicrafts. **Sunshine Handicraft**, Jln Pandak Mayah, has a range of *songket* products and sarongs.

✪ What to do

Georgetown *p44, map p44*
Snorkelling and diving
Pulau Payar is usually accessed from Langkawi but trips also run from Penang. **East Marine Holidays**, 5 Lengkok Nun, Penang (for the office), T04-226 3022, www.eastmarine.com.my, runs dive trips (RM350) and snorkelling trips (RM250), including the return ferry and buffet lunch.

Tour operators

The 3 main tours offered by companies are: the city tour; the Penang Hill and temple tour; and the round-the-island tour. All cost RM35-75 with 2 departures a day at 0900 and 1400. Most of the budget travel agents are along Lebuh Chulia. Several agencies around the Swettenham Pier. **Everrise Tours & Travel**, Lot 323, 2nd floor, Wisma Central, 202 Jl, T04-226 4329. **Georgetown Tourist Service**, Jln Imigresen, T04-229 5788, city island tours. **MS Star Travel Agencies**, 475 Lebuh Chulia, T04-262 2906. **MSL Travel**, Ming Court Inn Lobby, Jln Macalister, T04-227 2655 or 340 Lebuh Chulia, T04-261 6154, student and youth travel bureau. **Renae Agency**, 2 Penang Port Commission Complex, T04-262 2369. **Tour and Incentive Travel**, Suite 7B, 7th floor Menara BHL, Jln Sultan Ahmad Shah, T04-227 4522.

⊖ Transport

Tanah Rata *p38*

If you suffer from travel sickness take anti-nausea medication before setting out on the mountain road.

Bus

It is best to book in advance for all buses. The bus station is open 0730-1800. **Kurnia Bistari** has 5 express buses that run between **KL**'s Puduraya terminal and the Cameron Highlands, 0900-1530 (4½ hrs). Most other buses for the Cameron Highlands leave from **Tapah**, 67 km from Tanah Rata. There are connections every hour 0630-1830 with **Ringlet**, **Brinchang** and **Tanah Rata**. Tickets for the return journey can be booked at travel agents or at the bus station in Tanah Rata. From **Tapah** there are express buses to **KL** every 2 hrs 1020-1815. There are 4 express buses to **Ipoh** at 0800, 1100 and 1500 and 1800. There are 5 daily buses to **Penang**. For the east, it is necessary to travel to **Ipoh** and then change buses. Through tickets can

be purchased in Tanah Rata for **Kuantan** and **Kota Baru**. There is a daily bus to **Singapore** departing at 1000.

Car hire

Ravi, Rainbow Garden Centre (between The Smokehouse and Tanah Rata), T05-491782. Sound your horn at bends and beware of the lorries hurtling along.

Taxi

Taxis can be chartered for individual journeys or by the hour, or grab a seat in a shared taxi between **Tanah Rata** and **Brinchang**. Taxi and local bus station (T05-491 1485) on either side of the Shell station in Tanah Rata. To order a taxi, T05-491 1234.

Train

The nearest station is **Tapah**, 67 km from Tanah Rata. There is a daily connection with **Ipoh**. From Ipoh it is necessary to change trains for connections to **Butterworth** (4 daily, 1103, 1757, 0043 and 0107) and **Hat Yai** (once daily at 0043). There are 2 daily departures for **KL** (0119 and 1049). It is more convenient to take the bus to Ipoh and hop onto a train from there rather than starting the journey from Tapah.

Brinchang and around *p38*
Bus

Buses run between Tanah Rata, Brinchang and Tapah, or take a taxi (RM15).

Taxi

Taxis are available for local travel and can be chartered for about RM20 per hr.

Ipoh and around *p38*
Air

Sultan Azlan Shah Airport, T05-312 2459, 15 km south of town, RM25 taxi ride. Frequent connections with **Singapore** on Firefly.

Airline offices MAS, Lot 108 Bangunan Seri Kinta, Jln Sultan Idris Shah, T05-241 4155.

Bus

Ipoh is on the main north–south road and is well connected. The long-distance bus terminal **Medan Gopeng** is 4 km out of town, a RM10-12 taxi trip. Buses to **Taiping** (RM7), **Lumut** (RM6.50), **Cameron Highlands** (2 hrs, RM8) and **Kuala Kangsar** (RM5) leave from the local bus terminal which is 200 m from the railway station. Regular buses from Medan Gopeng to **Butterworth** (RM13.90), **KL** (RM17, 3 hrs), **Penang** (2½ hrs, RM13.90), **Alor Star** (RM22), **Kuantan**, **Sungai Petani**, **Johor Bahru**, **Kangar**, **Kuala Perlis**, **Kota Bharu** via Grik/Gerik. Sri Maju express coach company has a booking office at 2 Jln Bendahara, T05-253 5367. It operates a daily service to **Singapore** (RM52), **Johor Bahru** (RM44), **KL**, **Butterworth**, **Penang**, **Lumut**, **Alor Star** and **Kuala Kangsar**.

Star Shuttle (www.starwira.com) offers bus services to **KLIA** and the **LCCT**, with departures leaving from Bercham and Medan Gopeng every few hours round the clock. The journey takes around 4 hrs, RM42.

Car hire

Avis, at the airport, T05-206586; Hertz, Royal Casuarina Hotel, 18 Jln Gopeng, T05-250 5533, and at airport, T05-312 7109.

Taxi

Nam Taxi Company, 15 Jln Raja Mus Aziz, T05-241 2189; Radiocab, T05-254 0241. Shared taxis leave from beside the bus station for **KL**, **Butterworth**, **Taiping**, **Alor Star** and **Tapah**. Connections with **Hat Yai** in Thailand.

Train

Ipoh is on the main north–south line. 4 daily connections north with **Butterworth** (1103, 1757, 0043 and 0107, 5½ hrs) and 1 daily departure to **Hat Yai** at 0043 and 4 daily going south to **KL** (0217, 0341, 1128, 1910, 4 hrs). The 1128 service goes all the way to **Singapore**, 10 hrs, T05-254 7987.

Kuala Kangsar *p40*
Bus

The station is on Jln Raja Bendahara. Regular connections with **Ipoh**, **Butterworth**, **KL**, **Lumut**, **Taiping** and **Kota Bharu**.

Taxi

The only local transport. Shared taxis congregate by the bus station and run to **Butterworth**, **KL**, **Ipoh** and **Taiping** when full.

Train

The station is out of town to the northeast, on Jln Sultan Idris. Trains on the **KL–Butterworth** route stop here.

Taiping *p40*
Bus

The main long-distance bus station is 7 km out of town; take a bus or taxi. Regular connections with **Butterworth**, **Ipoh** and **KL**. Also a morning bus to **Kuantan** on the east coast. For other connections, change at Ipoh. Local buses for **Ipoh** and **Kuala Kangsar** run from the central bus station at Jln Masjid/Jln Iskandar.

Train

The station is on the west side of town. There are twice daily connections with **Ipoh**, **KL** and **Butterworth**.

Lumut *p41*
Bus

The bus station is in the centre of town, a few mins' walk from the jetty. Buses to **Ipoh** (every 30 mins, 1 hr 45 mins), **KL** and **Butterworth**. Less regular connections with **Melaka**. Buses also run to **Singapore**.

Boat

Ferries leave from Lumut jetty. Connections every 30 mins to **Pangkor** jetty (30 mins, RM10 one-way, 1st boat from Lumut at 0645, last boat at 2030; from Pangkor, 1st departure at 0645, last at 2030), also regular connections with **Pangkor Island Beach Resort**, jetty close to Golden Sands (RM12 one-way).

Taxi
Services to **Ipoh**, **KL** and **Butterworth**.

Pulau Pangkor *p41*
Boat
Ferries leave from **Lumut** jetty (lots of touts). Connections every 30 mins to Pangkor jetty (RM10 one-way, 30 mins from Lumut 0645-2030; from Pangkor 0645-2030), also regular connections from **Pangkor Island Beach Resort**, jetty close to Golden Sands (RM6 one-way). There are inter-island ferries or it is possible to hire fishing boats.

Bus/taxi
There is a fleet of pink minibus taxis from Pangkor village to other parts of the island. Prices are fixed.

Georgetown *p44, map p44*
Air
Penang International Airport lies 20 km south of Georgetown and 36 km from Batu Ferringhi, T04-643 4411. Transport to airport: 30 mins, RM38. Regular bus service from airport to Georgetown and Batu Ferringhi. Regular flights to **Johor Bahru**, **KL**, **Kota Kinabalu**, **Kuching** and **Langkawi**. International connections with **Bangkok**, **Phuket**, **Macau**, **Hong Kong**, **Jakarta**, **Surabaya**, **Medan** and **Singapore**. Firefly (www.fireflyz.com) has regular connections to **Langkawi**, **Subang**, **Kuantan**, **Kuala Terrenganu**, **Kota Bahru**, **Phuket**, **Medan** and **Banda Aceh**. Jet Star (www.jetstar.com) and Tiger Airways (www.tigerairways.com) also have regular flights to **Singapore**.

MAS has regular direct connections to **Singapore**, **Bangkok**, **Hong Kong**, **Jakarta** and **Medan**.

Airline offices AirAsia, 332 Lebuh Chulia T04-261 5642, with computers for online booking in air-conditioned comfort; **Cathay Pacific**, AIA Building, Lebuh Farquhar, T04-226 0411, **MAS, KOMTAR**, T04-262 0011 or at the airport, T04-643 0811; **Singapore Airlines**, Wisma Penang Gardens, 42 Jln Sultan Ahmad Shah, T04-226 3201; **Thai International**, Wisma Central, 202 Jln Macalister, T04-226 6000.

Boat
Passenger and car ferries operate from adjacent terminals, Pengkalan Raja Tun Uda, T04-331 5780. Ferry service between Georgetown and **Butterworth**. Ferries leave every 20 mins 0600-0100, RM1.20 one-way. Car RM7.70, motorbike RM2. **Selasa Express Ferry Company** has its office by the Penang Clocktower, next to the Penang Tourist Office, T04-262 5630. **Sejahtera** and **Fast Ferry Ventures** operate boats to **Langkawi** daily, 2 departures from each company a day, one at 0815 and another at 0830 (via **Pulau Payar**) (3 hrs), RM60 one-way (child RM45), RM115 return (child 85). Tickets can be bought from travel agents all over town. Boats leave from **Swettenham Pier**. You can take a motorcycle or bicycle aboard. Sadly, the ferry to **Medan** stopped running in 2010. Those travelling to Medan can now take one of the many flights over the Straits.

Bus
City buses leave from Lebuh Victoria near the **Butterworth** ferry terminal and serve Georgetown and surrounding areas. Buses around the island leave from **Pengkalan Weld** (Weld Quay) – next to the ferry terminal; all stop at KOMTAR. For schedules and routes check www.rapidpg.com.my.

Long distance The bus terminal is 7 km to the south of Georgetown at Sungai Nibong. The taxi ride there is a negotiable RM25. However, some buses depart from KOMTAR and head to the terminal at Butterworth and do not call at Sungai Nibong. Check where your bus departs from. Booking offices along Lebuh Chulia and inside KOMTAR. Some coaches operate from Pengkalan Weld direct to major towns on the Peninsula (see Butterworth, page 47). **Masa Mara Travel**, 54/4 Jln Burmah, is an agent for direct express buses from Penang to **Kota Bharu** (RM37.40) and **KL** (RM35, 5 hrs). Buses also ply the routes to **JB**, **Singapore**, **Melaka** and **Ipoh**. Minibus companies organize pick-ups from your hotel to **Hat Yai**, for connections north to Thailand. Pick-ups at 0500, 0830, 1200 and 1600. Other destinations include a change of bus at Hat Yai – **Bangkok** (18 hrs, RM120), **Surat Thani** (8 hrs, RM65) and **Phuket** (10 hrs, RM80). Some hotels (eg **Star Lodge** and **Cathay**) organize minibuses to Thailand. There is also an overnight bus to **Singapore**.

Car hire

Penang to **KL** by road is 4½ hrs. There is a one-way RM7 toll to drive across the bridge to the mainland. Many companies also have offices at the airport. **Budget**, 28 Jln Penang, T04-643 6025; **Hawk Rent-a-car**, T04-881 3886; **Hertz**, 38 Lebuh Farquhar, T04-263 5914; **New Bob Rent-a-Car**, 7/F Gottlieb Rd, T04-229 1111; **Orix**, City Bayview Hotel, 25A Lebuh Farquhar, T1800-881555.

Taxi

Long-distance taxis to all destinations on the Peninsula operate from the depot beside the Butterworth ferry on Pengkalan Weld. There are taxi stands on Jln Dr Lim Chwee Leong, Pengkalan Weld and Jln Magazine. No meters; agree price before setting off; short distances in city RM8-16. **Radio taxis**, T04-890 9918 (at ferry terminal); **CT Radio Taxi Service**, T04-229 9467. Taxis to Thailand: these run overnight to **Hat Yai** at the border; and from there to **Surat Thani** for Koh Samui; or **Krabi** for Phuket.

Train

The nearest station is by Butterworth ferry terminal, T04-261 0290. Book in advance for onward rail journeys at the station or ferry terminal, Pengkalan Weld, Georgetown.

From Butterworth: 2 daily to **Alor Star**, **Taiping**, **Ipoh**, **KL** (6 hrs) and **JB**. Also see Butterworth, below.

Around the Island *p46*
Bus

Rapid Penang bus No 101 goes to **Batu Ferringhi/Teluk Bahang** from Pengkalan Weld (Weld Quay) or KOMTAR in **Georgetown**, every 30 mins, RM2, 30-40 mins.

Taxi

Stands on Batu Ferringhi (opposite Golden Sands Hotel). Some taxis operate on commission; call in advance to check rates. From airport to **Batu Ferringhi**, 40 mins, RM60.

Butterworth *p47*

Butterworth is the main transport hub for Penang, and buses/trains on the east coast.

Bus

The bus station is next to the ferry terminal. There are regular connections with many Peninsula towns. Buses leave at least every hour for **Kuala Kedah** (for the Langkawi ferry). There are also buses to **Keroh**, on the border with Thailand, from where it is possible to get Thai taxis to **Betong**.

Ferry

Ferries for pedestrians and cars and leave for **Georgetown** every 15-20 mins from 0600-0100. The 20-min trip costs RM1.20.

Taxi

These congregate next to the ferry terminal. If you take a taxi to Penang you must pay the taxi fare plus the toll for the bridge (RM7).

Train

The station is beside the Penang ferry terminal. There are 2 daily connections with **Alor Star** and Taiping, and 4 with **Ipoh**, **KL** and **JB**. Trains also run to **Bangkok** (1 daily at 1420, 19 hrs), **Hat Yai** (2 daily,

457 and 1420, 5 hrs) and **Singapore**
1 daily at 0800, 14 hrs).

Pulau Langkawi p47
Air
The airport is 20 km from Kuah, 8 km
from Pentai Cenang. Taxi to Kuah Jetty
or Pantai Cenang RM24; buy a coupon
in the airport. Frequent connections with
Subang and **Penang** with Firefly, **KLIA**
with MAS and AirAsia, and **Singapore**
with SilkAir and AirAsia.
   Airline offices MAS, Langkawi
Fair Mall, Persiaran Putra, T04-746
3000; SilkAir, c/o MAS, T04-292 3122;
AirAsia, T04-202 7777.

Boat
It is worth hiring a boat if you can get a
group together, RM200 per day. Many
beach hotels also run boat trips to the
islands. Ferries to Langkawi leave from
Kuala Perlis (1 hr 30 mins, RM18) and
Kuala Kedah (1½ hrs, RM23). Timetables
subject to seasonal change (fewer boats
Apr-Sep). Boats run to **Kuala Perlis** every
hour 0700-1900, RM18. To **Kuala Kedah**
every hour 0700-1900, RM23. To **Penang**,
2 departures daily (1430 and 1715), RM60.
Leaving Langkawi, there are ticket agents
at the ferry. Connections with **KL** are easiest
from Kuala Kedah. If heading east to **Kota
Bharu** take a ferry to Kuala Perlis. Qudrat
Bistari Agency, sells bus tickets, at counter
9 of the Kuah jetty.
   To Thailand Langkawi Ferry Services
and Labuan Express both have connections
with **Satun** in Thailand, 50 mins, RM30.
There are at least 3 ferries a day at 1100,
1330 and 1700. It is possible to buy
through-tickets in Langkawi to **Phuket**
(RM70), **Krabi** (RM55) and **Surat Thani**
(RM65) via Satun.

Bus
There are no local buses. It is a 6-hr journey
from KL to **Kuala Kedah**; from there, catch
the boat to Langkawi.

Car hire
Mayflower Acme, Pelangi Beach Resort,
Pantai Cenang, T04-911 001; **Tomo Express**,
14 Jln Pandak Maya 4, Pekan Kuah, T04-966
9252. Expect to pay RM80 per day.

Taxi
Fares are fixed. From the jetty to **Kuah**,
RM6, to **Pantai Cenang**, RM24, to **Datai
Bay**, RM32.

Kuala Perlis
Bus/taxi
From the ferry terminal. There are regular
connections with **Butterworth**, **Alor Star**, **KL**
(every hour 0900-2200), **Kota Bharu** (2 daily,
0800 and 1945) and **Pedang Besar**. High-
speed ferry: departs Kuala Perlis jetty every
hour 0700-1900 to **Pulau Langkawi**, 45 mins,
RM18. Last ferry to Kuala Perlis at 1900.

ⓘ Directory

Tanah Rata p38
Banks All banks are on Jln Besar. It is
also possible to change money at CS
Travel & Tours. **Internet** Almost all
hotels have internet. **Medical services**
Hospital: opposite gardens at north
end of town, on Jln Besar, T05-491 1966.
Police T05-491 1222, opposite gardens
at north end of town.

Brinchang and around p38
Banks Public Bank, next to Garden
Lodge. **Internet** Next to the Fong Lum,
2nd floor. **Police** Central Square. **Post
office** Opposite the Petronas petrol
station at north end of town.

Ipoh and around p38
Banks Several on Jln Sultan Idris
Shah and Jln Yang Kalsom; in the new
town many banks on Jln Sultan Yussuf.
Internet Infoweb Station, Jln Dato
Onn Jaafar, near Jln Sultan Idris Shah.
Post office Next to the train station,
Jln Panglima Bukit Gantang Wahab.

Taiping *p40*

Banks Many banks at crossroads of Jln Kota and Jln Sultan Abdullah. **Poly Travels**, 53 Jln Mesjid, and **Fulham Tours**, 25 Jln Kelab Cina, have foreign-exchange facilities. **Internet** Discover de Internet, 3 Jln Panggong Wayang, RM2.50 per hr. **Helm Computer Technology Centre**, Jln Kota. **Post office** Jln Barrack.

Georgetown *p44, map p44*

Banks Most banks are in or around the GPO area and Lebuh Pantai. Money changers are here too, and on Jln Masjid Kapitan Keling and Lebuh Pantai, close to the Immigration office. **Consulates** Indonesia, 467 Jln Burmah, T04-227 5141 (60-day visa available); **Thailand**, No 1, Jalan Tunku Abdul Rahman, T04-226 8029 (visas in 2 days); **UK**, Honorary Consul, T04-227 5336. **Immigration** Corner of Lebuh Light and Lebuh Pantai, T04-261 5122. **Internet** Several along Lebuh Chulia, RM3 per hr. **Post office** Lebuh Pitt.

Medical services General Hospital (government), Jln Residensi, T04-229 3333; **Lam Wah Ee Hospital** (private), 141 Jln Batu Lancang, T04-657 1888. **Telephone** Telecoms office (international), Jln Burmah.

Pulau Langkawi *p47*

Banks Just off the main street in Kuah. Money changers at the ferry terminal offer poor rates. **Noorul Ameen**, 2nd floor, 15 Jln Pandak Mayah, opposite taxi stand, offers the best rates. Money changers at Pantai Cenang and Pantai Tengah. There is a Maybank ATM in the Underwater World complex **Customs** T04-966 6227. **Immigration** T04-969 4005. **Internet** Several including Langkawi Online, Langkawi Plaza. **Post office** At jetty end of main road. Those with laptops can buy **Langkawi Winet** coupons for RM10 (24 hrs) and connect to the islandwide Wi-Fi network. Coupons are available at the convenience stores lining the road.

Southern Peninsula

Melaka is one of the Malaysian tourism industry's trump cards, thanks to its Portuguese, Dutch and British colonial history, its rich Peranakan (Straits Chinese) cultural heritage and its picturesque hinterland of rural Malay kampongs. The route south from Melaka is a pleasant but unremarkable drive through plantation country to Johor Bahru (JB), on the southernmost tip of the Peninsula.

It is a short hop across the causeway from JB to Singapore, and Malaysia's east coast islands and resorts are within easy reach. One of the most famous of these is Pulau Tioman, a large volcanic outcrop on the east coast with perfect strips of sandy beaches, good diving and snorkelling, forest trails, mountain hikes and, for the most part, a laid-back atmosphere.

Melaka and around → *For listings, see pages 71-79.*

Thanks to its strategic location on the strait that bears its name, Melaka was a rich, cosmopolitan port long before it fell victim to successive colonial invasions vying for its strategic locaction on the Straits. Its wealth and influence are now a thing of the past, and the city's colourful history is itself a major money-spinner for Malaysia's tourism industry. With its striking Dutch colonial core and bustling Chinatown, housing the oldest Chinese temple in Malaysia, there's plenty to keep visitors occupied. After years of campaigning, Melaka was awarded joint UNESCO World Heritage City status in 2008 with Georgetown, Penang.

Arriving in Melaka
Getting there Melaka airport is at Batu Berendam, 9 km out of town. There are frequent flights from Pekanbaru (Sumatra). Express buses ply the KL–Melaka (150 km) and Singapore–Melaka (250 km) routes. From KLIA and the LCCT there is a coach service direct to Melaka departing KLIA Level 1, Gate 4 and from the bus station at the LCCT four times a day (RM21.90, two hours, check www.bjaya.com/airport.html for timetable). If these departure times are not convenient it is possible to take a bus via Nilai to Seremban and from there board a coach direct to Melaka. The modern bus station, **Melaka Sentral**, is a few kilometres out of town on Jalan Tun Razak. Taxis are notorious for ripping off tourists as drivers refuse to use their meters. From the bus station to the centre of town should cost RM12-15. Guesthouse touts often hassle new arrivals but can be helpful for finding budget accommodation. There are daily ferry connections with Dumai in Sumatra. ▸▸ *See Transport, page 76.*

Getting around While Melaka is a largish town it is still possible to enjoy many of the sights on foot; bicycles are also available for hire from some of the guesthouses and shops in town. There is a town bus service: the No 17 bus runs from the bus station to historical Melaka and on to the Portuguese area. Of more use to visitors is the **Panorama Melaka**

hop-on/hop-off bus service (RM2 single journey/RM5 for all day usage). The two lines cover the major tourist attractions in the city and link the city with Melaka Sentral. Taxis are plentiful. Colourful trishaws are not part of Melaka's public transport system; they survive by providing a service to tourists.

The **Jerak Warisan Heritage Trail** starts near the bridge by the quayside on Jalan Kota and covers all the major cultural sights. The route crosses the bridge, to the Baba Nyonya Heritage Museum, takes in some temples on Jonker Street and then heads back across the bridge to Stadthuys, St Paul's Church, St Paul's Hill and the Porta de Santiago Independence Monument. For a handout on the trail, ask at the tourist office.

There are boat tours down the river through the original port area and past some of the old Dutch houses (see What to do, page 74). The river is a little pungent, but the 16th-century sanitation adds to the realism.

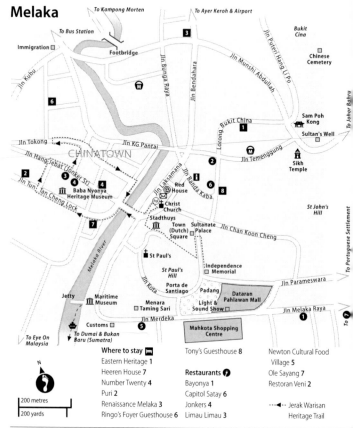

Melaka

Where to stay 🛏
Eastern Heritage 1
Heeren House 7
Number Twenty 4
Puri 2
Renaissance Melaka 3
Ringo's Foyer Guesthouse 6

Tony's Guesthouse 8

Restaurants 🍴
Bayonya 1
Capitol Satay 6
Jonkers 4
Limau Limau 3

Newton Cultural Food
Village 5
Ole Sayang 7
Restoran Veni 2

---◄--- Jerak Warisan
Heritage Trail

Tourist information Tourism Malaysia ① *Jln Banda Kaba (next to the Bangunan Tabung Haji office), T06-288 1549, Mon-Thu 0800-1300, 1400-1700, Fri 0800-1200, 1445-1700, closed Sat and Sun*, has good free maps. There is also a tourist information desk at **Ayer Keroh** ① *T06-293 3913*, and at **Melaka Sentral bus station** ① *T06-288 1340, www.tourism-melaka.com.*

Places in Melaka

Melaka's main sights of interest are on the eastern side of the river around Town Square (also known as Dutch Square). Behind the square St Paul's Hill rises above the town. On the other side of the river, Chinatown is lined with shophouses and antique shops. Jalan Hang Jebat (Jonker Walk) is closed off at weekends for the night market, which bustles with activity. Stalls are set up in front of shop houses, selling everything from toys to wooden clogs, while hawkers with pushcarts gather to sell delicious street food.

Town Square

The Dutch colonial architecture in Town Square is the most striking feature of the riverfront. The most prominent of these is the imposing **Stadthuys** (1660), said to be the oldest-surviving Dutch building in the East. Once the residence of Dutch governors, the building now houses a good **history museum** ① *Sat-Thu 0900-1730, Fri 0900-1215 and 1445-1730, RM5, free tours on Sat and Sun at 1030 and 1230*. Just opposite Stadthuys, **Christ Church** (1741-1753) ① *Thu-Tue*, is Malaysia's oldest Protestant church. The red bricks were shipped out from Zeeland in Holland and the floor is still studded with Dutch tombstones. The original pews are intact – as are its ceiling beams, each hewn from a single tree trunk more than 15 m long.

St Paul's Hill

Behind the gate at Stadthuys, a path leads up the hill to the ruins of **St Paul's Church** (1521), built on the site of the last Melakan sultans *istana*. From 1567-1596 the church was used as a fortress by the Portuguese, but it was badly damaged during the Dutch siege in 1641. The gravestones propped up in the interior and those strewn around the grounds provide a chilling remindeer of the diphtheria and cholera epidemics and early mortality that early settlers faced. There are good views of the city and the ruins now host buskers and souvenir sellers.

Head down the other side of the hill and you reach the **Porta de Santiago**, the remains of the great Portuguese fort **A Famosa**, said to have been built in four months flat under Admiral Alfonso d'Albuquerque's supervision in 1511. The fort sprawled across the whole hill and housed the entire Portuguese administration but it was virtually flattened by the British in 1806-1808 when they occupied Melaka during the Napoleonic Wars.

A wooden replica of Sultan Mansur Shah's 15th-century *istana* is below St Paul's. The **Sultanate Palace (Istana Ke Sultanan)** ① *daily 0900-1730, RM2*, was painstakingly reconstructed in 1985 using traditional techniques and materials. The magnificent palace was destroyed by fire after being struck by lightning the year after Mansur's accession.

Once the social centre of British colonial Melaka, the **Independence Memorial** ① *Sat-Thu 0900-1800, Fri 0900-1200 and 1500-1800, free*, now houses an extensive timeline exhibition covering Malaysia's journey to independence.

A brief history of Melaka

Melaka was founded at the end of the 14th century by a fugitive Hindu prince from Sumatra called Parameswara. Parameswara recognized the fishing kampong's strategic potential: it was sheltered from the monsoons by the island of Sumatra and perfectly located for merchants to take advantage of the trade winds. What's more, because the strait's deep-water channel lay close to the Malayan coast, Melaka had command over the ships passing through it. The settlement became wealthy by trading spices and textiles with Indonesia and India. Taxes levied on imported goods rapidly made it into one of the richest kingdoms in the world.

In 1405, the Chinese, who already had a sophisticated trade network linking Asia, India, the Middle East and Europe, sent an envoy, Cheng Ho, bearing gifts from the Ming emperor (including a yellow parasol, which has been the emblem of Malay royalty ever since). They offered to help protect Melaka from the Siamese in exchange for using it as a supply base. The Chinese that settled became known as Straits Chinese or Nyonya.

Indian merchants also arrived. They sometimes had to wait several months before the winds changed to allow them to return home. Consequently, many of them put down roots in Melaka and permanent Indian communities developed.

Ever keen to consolidate trade links, the third ruler of Melaka, Sri Maharaja, married the daughter of the sultan of the thriving state of Sumudra-Pasai, Sumatra. In so doing, he embraced Islam and "hitched Melaka's fortunes to the rising star of Muslim trading fraternity" (Mary Turnbull). It was made the state religion and spread through the merchant community.

For three centuries Melaka was at the fulcrum of the Asian trade route and was known as the emporium of the East. Foreign merchants traded in textiles, silk, spices, porcelain, gold, pepper, camphor, sandalwood and tin. By the 16th century, tales of luxury and prosperity attracted the Portuguese, who came in search of trading opportunities, with the aim of breaking the Arab merchants' stranglehold on trade between Europe and Asia. Alfonso d'Albuquerque stormed and conquered the city in 1511, with 18 ships and 1400 men. The sultan fled to Johor to re-establish his kingdom.

The Portuguese occupiers stayed for 130 years but back in Lisbon the monarchy was on the decline and the government in serious debt; the Portuguese never managed to subdue the Sumatran pirates, the real rulers of the Strait of Melaka.

Taking advantage of this weakness, the Dutch entered an alliance with the Sultanate of Johor and, in 1641, after a six-month siege of the city, they forced the surrender of the last Portuguese governor. Over the next 150 years, the Dutch carried out an extensive building programme, some of these, including the red building of Stadhuys, still stand on Dutch Square.

By the late 18th century the English East India Company wanted a share of the action. In 1829, Melaka was ceded to the British in exchange for the Sumatran port of Bencoolen. It became part of the British Straits Settlements but went into decline as the administration was moved to Singapore. This proved to be its saving grace and it suffered little damage during the Second World War.

In 2008, Melaka was awarded UNESCO World Heritage City Status, together with Georgetown, Penang, as Historic Cities of the Straits of Malacca.

East bank

The **Maritime Museum** ① *on the riverbank, 200 m from the river boat embarkation point, Mon-Thu 0900-1730, Fri-Sun 0900-2030, RM3,* is housed in a full-scale reconstruction of the Portuguese trading vessel *Flor de la Mar* – thought to be the richest ship ever lost. This is one of the best museums in Melaka, given its history of sea trade. It has a collection of models of foreign ships that docked at Melaka during its maritime supremacy from the 14th century to the Portuguese era.

Menara Taming Sari ① *Jln Merdeka, Bandar Hilir, T06-288 1100, www.menaratamingsari.com, daily 1000-2200, RM20, RM10 child,* is a rather ugly blot on the landscape towering above the Dataran Pahlawan. This is yet another Malaysian record breaker, and is registered as the First Revolving Gyro Tower in Malaysia. The cabin takes groups of tourists up to a height of 80 m and then slowly turns a full circle before descending. Good views over the city.

Chinatown

From Dutch Square, a concrete bridge leads to the picturesque **Jalan Tun Tan Cheng Lock**. It is lined with the Straits Chinese community's ancestral homes and is Melaka's Millionaires' Row. Many of the houses have intricately carved doors that were often specially built by immigrant craftsmen from China. Today tour buses exacerbate the local traffic problem, which clogs the narrow one-way street, but many of its Peranakan mansions are still lived in by the same families that built them in the 19th century.

One of the most opulent of these houses has been converted into the **Baba Nyonya Heritage Museum** ① *48-50 Jln Tun Tan Cheng Lock, T06-283 1273, daily 1000-1230 and 1400-1630, RM8 adult, RM4 child.* It is in a well-preserved traditional Peranakan town house, built in 1896 by millionaire rubber planter Chan Cheng Siew. The house contains family heirlooms and antiques, including Nyonya porcelain and blackwood furniture with marble or mother-of-pearl inlay, and silverware. Tours run regularly throughout the day.

West bank

On the west bank is **Kampong Morten**, a village of traditional Melakan houses. It was named after a man who built Melaka's wet market and donated the land to the Malays. The main attraction here is Kassim Mahmood's handcrafted house.

North Melaka

In 1460 when Sultan Mansur Shah married Li Poh, a Ming princess, she took up residence on Melaka's highest hill, **Bukit Cina**, which became the Chinese quarter. It is now the largest traditional Chinese burial ground outside China, containing more than 12,000 graves, some of which date back to the Ming Dynasty.

At the foot of the hill is an old Chinese temple called **Sam Poh Kong**, dedicated to the famous Chinese seafarer, Admiral Cheng Ho. It was originally built to cater for those whose relatives were buried on Bukit Cina. This temple has a peaceful and relaxed atmosphere and is interesting to explore.

Portuguese Settlement (Ujong Pasir)

① *3 km east of town, take a Panorama Melaka bus from outside Stadthuys or Mahkota Parade.* Ujong Pasir has been a Portuguese settlement for nearly five centuries. Unlike the Dutch and British colonial regimes, the Portuguese garrison was encouraged to integrate and inter-marry with the Malays. The process of integration was so successful that when the

Dutch, after capturing the city in 1641, offered Portuguese settlers a choice between amnesty and deportation to their nearest colony, many chose to stay. In the 1920s they were allotted a small area of swampland and the settlement visible today was built, its streets named after Portuguese heroes largely unrecognized in Malaysia. The main square, built only in 1985, is a concrete replica of a square in Lisbon and is visibly ersatz. Today these Portuguese Malaysians number around 2600 (10,000 in Malaysia).

Johor Bahru → *For listings, see pages 71-79. Phone code: 07.*

Modern Johor Bahru, more commonly called JB, is not a pretty town. It lies on the southernmost tip of the Peninsula and is the gateway to Malaysia from Singapore. JB is short on tourist attractions but has for many years served either as a tacky red-light reprieve for Singaporeans and/or as a large retail outlet. There is little reason to stay here; most travellers pass through on their way from or to Singapore.

If you are in town, it's worth visiting the **Istana Besar**. Built by Sultan Abu Bakar in 1866, it is a slice of Victorian England set in beautiful gardens, overlooking the strait. It now houses the **Royal Abu Bakar Museum** ① *Jln Tun Dr Ismail, T07-223 0555, closed for renovations at the time of research but should be open again by the time you read this.* In the north wing is the throne room and museum containing a superb collection of royal treasures, including gruesome hunting trophies such as hollow elephant feet and an array of tusks and skulls, as well as Chinese and Japanese ceramics.

Arriving in Johor Bahru

Senai Airport ① *20 km from town, www.senaiairport.com*, has connections with KL, Subang, Kuching, Kota Kinabalu, Miri, Penang and Sibu. The growth of budget operators flying out of Changi has had a significantly detrimental effect on Senai, signalling the end of international routes departing from here. A shuttle bus runs into town. There is a regular bus service between Singapore and KL. The KL Singapore railway line runs through JB. There is a **FerryLink** service between Changi Point in Singapore and Tanjung Belungkor in the eastern corner of Johor state. This has the advantage of avoiding the congested causeway across the border. Car hire in JB is cheaper than in Singapore. Cheap taxis (meters not an option) provide the main form of transport. ▶▶ *See Transport, page 76.*

There are two tourist offices at 2 Jalan Air Molek: **JOTIC** ① *T07-224 9960, www. johortourism.com.my, Mon-Fri 0800-1630, Sat 0800-1230*, and the **Tourism Malaysia Information Centre** ① *T07-222 3591, www.tourismmalaysia.com.my*.

Pulau Tioman and around → *For listings, see pages 71-79.*

There are a total of 64 islands in the volcanic Seribuat archipelago, off Malaysia's east coast. Many are inaccessible and uninhabited. The most popular is Tioman, made famous by the Hollywood movie *South Pacific*, which has scores of resorts, simple beach huts and dive operators. It is also possibly to island hop to bask on deserted beaches or snorkel in coves.

Pulau Tioman → *Phone code: 07*

Tioman, 56 km off Mersing, is the largest island in the archipelago at 20 km by 12 km. The interior is dominated by several jagged peaks and is densely forested, while its coast is fringed by white-sand beaches and traditional fishing kampongs. Despite development many of these kampongs have retained their scruffy charm and are still very laid back.

Thankfully, as yet, there are no nightclubs or fast-food restaurants and the tourist shops are very low key.

Most of the island's inhabitants live on the west side of the island. The main village, **Tekek**, is where most passengers arrive and has most of the island's facilities including shops, a post office, police post, clinic, money changes and an immigration office. Most of the accommodation is a five- to 10-minute walk south of the jetty, but much of it is run down. The beach is rocky at low tide at **Ayer Batang** (also known as ABC) and the sandy area quite small. There are a couple of mini markets for supplies and souvenirs, a small beach bar and internet. **Kampong Salang** is the northernmost development on the island and is set in a sheltered cove with a beautiful beach. The beach is more rowdy than Ayer Batang, with concrete development and more of a party scene, popular with

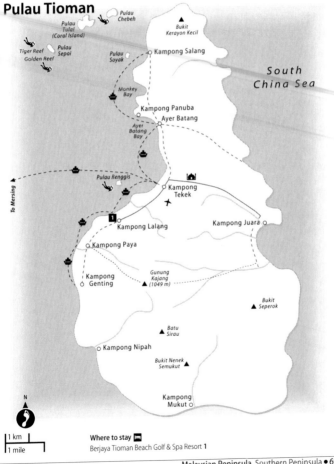

Pulau Tioman

Pulau Chebeh

Pulau Tulal (Coral Island)

Tiger Reef
Golden Reef

Pulau Sepoi

Pulau Soyak

Bukit Kerayon Kecil

▲ Kampong Salang

South China Sea

Monkey Bay

Kampong Panuba
Ayer Batang

Ayer Batang Bay

To Mersing

Pulau Renggis

Kampong Tekek

Kampong Lalang

1

Kampong Juara

Kampong Paya

Gunung Kajang ▲ (1049 m)

Kampong Genting

Bukit ▲ Seperok

▲ Batu Sirau

Kampong Nipah

Bukit Nenek ▲ Semukut

Kampong Mukut

N

| 1 km |
| 1 mile |

Where to stay 🛏
Berjaya Tioman Beach Golf & Spa Resort **1**

backpackers. The island is virtually uninhabited on the southeast and southwest sides with the kampongs of **Nipah** and **Mukut** just starting to open up to tourism. The only place to stay on the east of the island is **Juara**, which has a beautiful long white beach and good breakers (no good for snorkelling). Being on the seaward side, Juara has a different atmosphere from the west coast kampongs; it is quieter, friendlier, more laid back and bucolic, thanks mainly to its seclusion.

Visiting Pulau Tioman   The airport is in the centre of Tekek and has daily connections with KL and Singapore. The jetty is 100 m away where you can catch a sea taxi or ferry. Most people arrive on Tioman by ferry from Mersing (see Transport, page 77). The website www.tiomanisland.com.my, has lots of useful information.

There are very few trails around the island and one main road. You can walk from the west side of the island to the east by a beautiful jungle trail (see What to do, page 75) or hire a taxi in town, preferably 4WD. To get from one kampong to another, it's best to take the sea taxi service that works its way around the island. To get to Mukut and Nipah you must get off at Genting from where you can hire a boat to the beach. For Paya you need to ask the boat to make the stop.

Many locals are unhappy with the sale of alcohol on the island. However, the upmarket resorts generally cater to alcohol-drinking guests and there is plenty of cheap booze at the duty-free stores. Many of the simpler chalet operations do not allow alcohol on their premises, while a few others will quietly serve beer or wine at their restaurant.

For diving the best time is February to September to avoid the rainy season. During the monsoon (November to March), the seas are very rough and many island resorts are closed. May to September is best for turtle spotting. ▶▶ *See What to do, page 75.*

Other islands

There is accommodation on Pulau Rawa, Pulau Babi Besar (Big Pig Island), Pulau Tinggi, Pulau Sibu, Pulau Aur (Bamboo Island) and Pulau Pemanggil. **Sibu** is the most popular and is recommended for its beaches and watersports. Once a pirate haunt, Sibu is frequented more by Singaporeans and expats than by Western tourists. It is popular for fishing, diving and walking because it is larger than the other islands there is more of a sense of space.

Mersing

This small fishing port is a pleasant little town distinguished only by the Masjid Jamek, a green-tiled mosque, on top of a hill. Most people are in a hurry to get to the islands, namely Pulau Tioman, but ferry times can be erratic, so you may need to stay here overnight. It's a pleasant enough place, with some good restaurants, a shiny new shopping plaza and a plethora of ticketing agencies. **Mersing Tourist Information Centre** ⓘ *Jln Abu Bakar, T07-799 5212, Mon-Thu 0800-1300 and 1400-1630, Fri 0800-1200 and 1445-1630, Sat 0800-1245,* is a useful source of information.

Southern Peninsula listings

For hotel and restaurant price codes and other relevant information, see pages 9-11.

⚫ Where to stay

Melaka and around *p63, map p64*

There are lots of upmarket hotels around Tanjung Kling; good budget options can be found around Taman Melaka Raya. Booking in advance is a good idea for weekend visits.

$$$$ Renaissance Melaka, Jln Bendahara, T06-284 8888, www.marriott.com. 24 storeys high, it is the tallest building in the town. With 300 rooms, all of which are spacious and elegantly appointed with Malaccan wood furniture, a/c, mini-fridge, TV, in-house video and grand views either over the town or to the sea. Also coffee shop, restaurants, fitness centre, pool on the 9th floor.

$$ Heeren House, 1 Jln Tun Tan Cheng Lock, T06-281 4241, www.heerenhouse. com. Charm galore can be found at this riverside guesthouse with comfy Peranakan- and colonial-style rooms, excellent management and oodles of ambience. English breakfast included. Free Wi-Fi. Recommended.

$$ Number Twenty, 20 Jln Hang Jebat, T06-281 9761, www.twentymelaka.com. Charming guesthouse housed in a Dutch edifice built in 1673. With high ceilings, exposed beams and creaking floorboards there are plenty of ancient vibes, although the owners have managed to blend these features well with simple contemporary furnishings. Rooms are a/c and have Wi-Fi access. Breakfast included. The downside of this location is the Malay karaoke that blares from next door until late.

$$ Puri, 118 Jln Tun Tan Cheng Lock, T06-282 5588, www.hotelpuri.com. Beautiful hotel in a restored Peranakan house, with a Chinese garden café and a lobby with a piano and spiral staircase. Rooms are clean and tastefully furnished; several have balconies. Wi-Fi. Breakfast included.

$ Eastern Heritage, 8 Jln Bukit China, T06-283 3026, www.eastern-heritage.com. Great old Chinese building with carved wood and gold inlay, spacious rooms on 2nd floor, dorm on 3rd floor, small dipping pool on 1st floor, batik lessons, good location. Popular, with an authentic feel.

$ Ringo's Foyer Guesthouse, 46A Jln Portugis, T06-281 6393, www.ringosfoyer. com.my. Highly social place owned by a local musician and his pals, the rooms are basic but clean and have a/c or fan with shared bathroom. The guesthouse is festooned with items salvaged from the dump, and they have made excellent use of old sewing machines, windows and doorways throughout. Pleasant rooftop terrace for beers and sunbathing. Howard, one of the owners, takes guests out each night to sample Melaka's cuisine. Single sex dorms (RM13). Wi-Fi. Recommended

$ Tony's Guesthouse, 24 Lorong Banda Kaba, T012-688 0119, cobia43@hotmail. com. While this place is a bit tatty, it offers cheap fan rooms, a helpful owner and free Wi-Fi. Rooms are eye bulgingly colourful and covered in Tony's eccentric art. Shared bathrooms.

Johor Bahru *p68*

JB's top hotels cater for business people and have all the 5-star facilities. Most budget travellers don't stop in JB so there really isn't much choice, except for short-stay hotels.

$ Causeway Inn, 6 Jln Meldrum, T07-224 8811. A/c, clean, quiet, well-run, smart hotel that does not overcharge. TV, excellent bathroom. Ask for a room with views.

$ Top, 12 Jln Meldrum, T07-224 4755. Much better value than most. Large rooms with huge beds. Very good bathrooms.

Pulau Tioman *p68, map p69*

Most accommodation on the island is simple, with home-cooked meals. Sandflies can be a problem so take mosquito coils. Expect to pay more for mosquito nets and electricity. Inevitably, beachfront chalets cost more. Due to stiff competition, many prices are negotiable. For more luxurious resorts, check their websites in advance for specials deals; you can find some real bargains, especially in low season. Be wary of buying the much proffered packages from travel agents in Mersing. Better deals are to be had on the island, despite what the agents claim.

$$$-$$ Nazri's Place, T07-419 1329, www.nazrisplace.com. The most southerly of the guesthouses in Ayer Batang. There's a concrete block with tiled rooms with a/c, and some huts at the back of the plot, among the mango trees. Spartan but clean rooms, sea-front restaurant, friendly management, good discounts during low season. Best stretch of beach in Ayer Batang. Recommended.

$$$-$ Babura Sea View, Kampong Tekek, south end of the beach, T07-419 1139, www.baburaseaview.com. The 23 rooms are clean and well maintained; the best are in the newish block on the beachfront. Some a/c, restaurant. Good Chinese restaurant, and **Tioman Reef Divers**, a PADI/NAUI dive shop.

$$ Bamboo Hill Chalets, T09-419 1339, www.bamboohillchalets.com. Selection of fan and a/c chalets at the far end of the beach, some perched on a hilltop overlooking the bay. The chalets are well designed and comfortable and have hot-water showers and balconies with sea views. Small library and water refilling service (RM1).This place is extremely popular and advance booking is essential. Recommended.

$$ Salang Sayang (also known as **Zaids Place's**), T09-419 5019, www.salangsayang resort.com. Well-managed resort with a wide selection of comfortable a/c and fan chalets, many with sea view and some perched regally on a hillside overlooking the swaying palms. The top rooms here are the concrete a/c suites, with fridge, kettle, narcolepsy inducing beds and sea views. Excellent package deals available for advanced bookings. Recommended.

$ ABC Bungalows, Ayer Batang, T07-419 1154. Popular place to stay at the northern end of the stretch, with some good snorkelling. Small A-frames, attractive little plot with family atmosphere, good cheap food, hammocks, volleyball, friendly service.

$ Lagoon and Riverview Place, Kampong Juara, T09-419 3168 (Riverview), T09-419 3153 (Lagoon), www.riverview-tioman. com. The cheapest yet most scenic places to stay between an aquamarine mangrove swamp and the Sungai Baru River at the northern edge of the bay. Simple chalets right on the beach. Also serves some of the best seafood.

$ Nazri's Place II, Ayer Batang, www.nazris place.com. Decent, clean and not too cramped rooms with wooden floors and sea views. A raised restaurant provides a spectacular view of the bay. Laundry service, jet skiing, fishing and snorkelling available.

$ Paradise Point, Kampong Juara. One of only 3 places to stay on the northern side of the beach. Simple rooms, attached showers, the chalets closest to the beach get the breeze, a quiet place with a relaxed atmosphere. Restaurant with extensive menu

$ Tekek Inn, T07-419 1576. Perhaps the best of the cheaper places to stay. It is on the beach, rooms are OK with attached showers and there are snorkels and canoes for hire.

Other islands *p70*

$$$ Sea Gypsy Village Resort, Pulau Sibu, T07-222 8642, www.siburesort.com. Restaurant, chalets and bungalows. Friendly. The company also works with a dugong conservation project. Offers good transport options from Singapore and JB.

$ O & H Kampong Huts, Pulau Sibu, c/o 9 Tourist Information Centre, Jln Abu Bakar, Mersing, T07-799 3124. Good restaurant, chalets, some with attached bathrooms, clean and friendly, trekking and snorkelling.

Mersing *p70*

$$ Mersing Inn, 38 Jln Ismail, T07-799 1919. A 5-min walk from the jetty, this spotless but wholly unexciting hotel has a range of comfortable carpeted a/c rooms with attached bathroom and tiny TV.

$$ Seri Malaysia, Jln Ismail, T07-799 1876, www.serimalaysia.com.my. Clean a/c rooms, limited ambience and fair prices.

$$ Timotel, 839 Jln Endau, T07-799 5898, www.timotel.com.my. Looks like a set of offices and is located near the long-distance bus stand, this hotel is a bit of a trek into town. Rooms are comfy and spacious, making this one of the town's better mid-range options.

$$-$ Embassy, 2 Jln Ismail, T07-799 3545. Selection of a/c and fan rooms with TV and attached bathroom in the heart of the town. The hotel is efficiently managed and kept spotlessly clean. Rooms at the front face a busy road and can be a bit noisy, ask for a room at the back. Recommended.

🍴 Restaurants

Melaka and around *p63, map p64*

$$ Jonkers, 17 Jln Hang Jebat. Closes 1600. Old Nyonya house, with restaurant in the old ancestral hall. Good atmosphere and excellent food – Nyonya and international, good-value set menu.

$$ Ole Sayang, 1988199 Taman Melaka Raya, T06-283 1966. Serves all the favourites in a twee fusion of tea room and standard Chinese restaurant. Menu includes chicken *pongteh*, *udang sambal*, and unbelievably good *itek tim* soup. Highly recommended.

$ Bayonya, 164 Taman Malaka Raya. Excellent Peranakan cuisine. Owned by an enthusiast who provides a culture lesson with your meal.

$ Capitol Satay, 41 Lorong Bukit Cina, T06-283 5508. It's better to arrive early at this highly popular place serving *sate celup*, meat on a sate stick cooked in a broth or scalding peanut sauce. Recommended. Get there before 1800 for a seat or face a long queue.

$ Limau Limau, 9 Jln Hang Lekiu. Relaxing café serving up superb sandwiches including hummus pitas and roasted vegetable ciabatta. The house salad featuring lychees is unusual, innovative and very tasty.

$ Restoran Veni, 34 Jln Temenggong, T06-284 9570. Open 0700-2200. Highly acclaimed eatery with superb veg and non-veg sets with daily veg specials. Good fish cutlets, extraordinarily zesty lime pickle and mountains of rice. Recommended.

Foodstalls

Reassuringly touristy and spotlessly clean, **Newton Cultural Food Village**, opposite the Menara Taming Sari has dangling red lanterns and a selection of well-priced stalls serving up Portuguese curries, *popiah*, Penang-fried *kway teow*, fish soups and even sushi. Open 1100-2200. Recommended.

Jln Semabok (after Bukit Cina on road to JB), Malay-run fish-head curry stall, a local favourite. **Klebang Beach**, off Jl Klebang Besar, Tanjung Kling – several *ikan panggang* (grilled fish) specialists.

Johor Bahru *p68*

$$$ Meisan, Mutiara Hotel, Jln Dato Sulaiman, Century Garden. Superb but expensive Sichuan restaurant, spicy specialities.

$$ Newsroom Café, Puteri Pacific Hotel, Jln Abdullah Ibrahim, T07-219 9999. Reasonably priced local and continental dishes.

$$ Seasons Cafi, branches in City Square and Plaza Pelangi. Café serving Western snacks and breads and Asian rice dishes.

Foodstalls

JB is known for its seafood. The **night market** on Jln Wong Ah Fook is a great place to sample the full array of stall dishes. **Tepian Tebrau**, Jln Skudam, has good satay and grilled fish. **Pantai Lido** is a well-known hawker centre.

Pulau Tioman *p68, map p69*
Most restaurants are small family-run kitchens attached to beach huts. All provide Western staples such as omelettes and French toast, as well as Malay dishes. On the whole, the food is of a high standard. Seafood is good and fresh: superb barbecued barracuda, squid, stingray and other fish.

Mersing *p70*
$$ Mersing Seafood, 56 Jln Ismail, T07-799 2550. Open 1100-1430, 1700-2330. One of Mersing's best spots for seafood lovers with an extensive menu of fresh squid, crab, prawns and fish served in a/c comfort. Highlights include sambal prawns, assam fish-head curry and fresh crab with black pepper sauce. Some vegetarian options.
$ Golden Dragon Restaurant, 2 Jln Ismail. Big Chinese seafood menu, reasonably priced, chilli crabs, drunken prawns, wild boar and *kangkong belacan*. Excellent banana/pineapple pancakes for breakfast.
$ Restoran P1, 20 Jln Dato Mohd Ali, T07-799 4603. Open 1120-1500, 1730-2400. Owned by the affable Urs from Switzerland, this unnasuming eatery offers tasty pizza, pasta, salads and ice cold beer for very reasonable prices.
$ Sin Nam Kee Seafood, 387 Jln Jemaluang, 1 km out of town on Kota Tinggi road. Huge seafood menu and reckoned by locals to be the best restaurant in Mersing. Occasional karaoke nights can be noisy.

🎵 Bars and clubs

Melaka and around *p63, map p64*
At weekends **Geographer's Café** and **Ringo's Classic Bar** (both Jln Lekir) get really busy and have a superb, bustling ambience. On the intersection of Jln Hang Lekir and Jln Tun Tan Cheng Lock is the **EZ and Light Bar**, a place popular with locals for after work beer and a game of pool. Backpackers congregate at the **Discovery Café**, although the awful live music drives them away soon enough.

🛒 Shopping

Melaka and around *p63, map p64*
Antiques Melaka is well known for its antique shops, which mainly sell European and Chinese items. **Jln Hang Jebat** (formerly Jonker St) is the best place, selling everything from shadow puppets to Melakan furniture inlaid with mother-of-pearl. Fri, Sat and Sun evenings see the whole street turned into a market with vendors selling everything from antique postcards, to glow in the dark stars and delightful lamps. The street is quiet on Mon. **Malacca Woodwork**, 312c Klebang Besar, T06-315 4468. Specialist in authentic reproduction antique furniture.

Handicrafts Crystal Dbeaute, 18 Medan Portugis. **Dulukala**, Jln Laksamana. A varied collection including prints and batiks. **Karyaneka** centres at 1 Jln Laksamana and Mini Malaysia Complex, Ayer Keroh.

Paintings Jonker Art Collection, 76 Jln Hang Jebat, T06-283 6578. A small shop selling prints by local artists, in particular the work of Titi Kwok, son of the well-known Macau-based artist Kwok Se and owner of the **Cheng Hoon Art Gallery** situated a couple of streets away on Jln Tokong. He is often in the shop selling his own beautiful Chinese-style ink paintings. Recommended. **Orang Utan House**, 59 Lorong Hang Jebat. Paintings by local artist Charles Cham. He has a couple of shops around town and designs some highly original T-shirts which are a bargain at RM30. Recommended. For more see www.charlescham.com.

⏰ What to do

Melaka and around *p63, map p64*
Boat tours of Melaka's docks, godowns, old Dutch trading houses, wharves and seafront markets run from the quay opposite Christ Church (typically RM15 for 45 mins). Guides

are informative, pointing out settlements and wildlife. There are views of the giant lizards on the banks and plenty of rubbish floating downstream. Boats leave when full and usually there is a departure every hour 1400-1700, depending on the tides. Tickets can be bought from the tourist office (45 mins, RM15). For bookings, T06-286 5468.

Pulau Tioman p68, map p69
Boats leave from Kampong Tekek to Pulau Tulai (Coral Island) Turtle Island, to a waterfall at Mukut or an around-island trip. If boats are not full the prices increases. Trips can also be arranged to other nearby islands.

Diving
There are dive shops based in most of the kampongs. Tioman's coral reefs are mainly on the western side of the island, although sadly large areas have been killed off due to damage by fishing boats, the crown-of-thorns starfish, pollution and coral harvesting.

There are still some magnificent coral beds within easy reach. **Pulau Renggis**, just off the Berjaya Tioman Beach Resort, is the most accessible coral from the shore, and is a good place for new divers. For more adventurous dives, the islands off the northwest coast offer more of a challenge. There is cave diving off **Pulau Chebeh** (up to 25 m) and varied marine life of the cliff-like rocks of the **Golden Reef** (up to 20 m) and nearby **Tiger Reef** (9-24 m). Off the northeastern tip of the island is **Magicienne Rock** (20-24 m dives), where bigger fish can be seen. Off the southwestern coast is **Bahara Rock** (20 m), considered one of the best spots on the island. Many divers rate the experience of swimming through gigantic gorgonian sea fans as one of their scuba highlights.

Hiking
The cross-island trail, from the mosque in Kampong Tekek to Kampong Juara, on the east coast, is a 2- to 3-hr hike

(4 km), which is quite steep in places. It is a great walk but for those planning to stay at Juara, it is a tough climb with a full pack. The trail winds its way through the jungle via a waterfall and an enchanting upland plateau with massive trees such as strangler figs. It is not unusual to see squirrels, monkeys, monitor lizards, shrews and tropical insects. From Tekek, follow the path past the airport and then turn inland towards the mosque. From Juara, the trail begins opposite the pier. Guides are available but the trail is well marked.

There are also many easier jungle and coastal walks along the west coast: south from Tekek, past the resort to kampongs **Paya** and **Genting** and north to **Salang**. The walk from Ayer Batang to Salang is a difficult one of more than 3 hrs, with a trail that snakes over rocky outcrops, fallen trees and sometimes peters out altogether. About 1½ hrs into the walk you will reach **Monkey Bay**, which is a beautiful white sandy beach. If you get fed up with the trek you can always ask a passing boatman to take you back to civilization. The sea taxi ride from Monkey Bay back to Penuba, ABC or Salang costs RM15. There are times that the trail gets very difficult to follow, and the best way is to keep following the power line above it, which runs between ABC and Salang. Bring enough water and don't attempt the walk in flip-flops.

Mersing p70
Boats for fishing trips can be chartered by groups of 12 or more from the jetty. Owners may be reluctant to make the long journey out to the far offshore islands.

Tour operators
Competition is intense at peak season and tourists can be hassled for custom. Prices tend to be similar, but it's best to use licensed agents (usually displayed on the door). Many agents are located in the R&R Plaza on Jln Tun Dr Ismail, next to the river. They also promote package deals to specific

chalet resorts; sometimes they are good value, but buying a boat ticket puts you under no obligation to stay at a particular place. Recommended agents include: **Dee Travel & Tours**, T07-799 2344, 8 Jln Abu Bakar; **Golden Mal Tours**, 9 Jln Sulaiman, T07-799 1463; **Island Connection Travel & Tours**, 2 Jln Jemaluang, T07-799 2535; **Pure Value Tours**, 7 Jln Abu Bakar T07-799 6811.

⊖ Transport

Melaka and around p63, map p64
Air
Airport is at Batu Berendam, 9 km out of town. **Riau Airlines** (www.riau-airlines. com) and **Wings Air** (www.lionair.co.id) offer frequent connections to **Pekanbaru** in Sumatra (a 5-hr bus ride from Bukittingi). Tickets cost around RM300 for the short flight. Tourists from EU countries, Japan, USA and Australia are currently eligible for a VOA (Visa On Arrival) at Pekanbaru Airport. Check with your nearest Indonesian embassy regarding any changes before purchasing a ticket.

Boat
Indomal Express ferries to **Dumai** (Sumatra), leave daily at 1000 from the public jetty on Melaka river, 2 hrs. Indomal Express office, G29, Jln PM10, Plaza Mahkota, T06-283 2506, www.m-sia.com/indomal/index.html. Tickets can also be bought from travel agents. Try **Atlas Travel Service**, Jln Hang Jebat, T06-282 0315. Service leaves Melaka at 1000, one-way RM110; return RM170.

Bus
Journeys around town cost roughly RM1 on local buses. The **Panorama Melaka** hop-on/hop-off buses do a circuit of the town calling at major tourist sights. There is a stop by Stadthuys. A ticket, valid for a whole day, costs RM5. There are are 2 routes, clearly marked at each stop. The blue route covers a larger area and passes Kampung Portugiss, Baba Nyonya Heritage Museum,

Bukit China and Melaka Sentral. The smaller red route cover the main tourist spots.

Long distance Buses leave from the **Melaka Sentral** bus terminal on Jln Tun Razak. Regular connections from Melaka Sentral with **KL** (RM12.30), **Seremban** (RM6.80), **Port Dickson** (RM3), **Ipoh** (RM29.60), **Butterworth** and **Penang** (RM40), **Lumut** (Pulau Pangkor), **Kuantan** (RM27.90), **Kuala Terengganu** (RM34.20), **Kota Bharu** (RM43.10), **Johor Bahru** (RM19.40) and **Singapore** (via JB, 4 hrs, RM22).

There is a 4 times daily shuttle service from Melaka calling in at **KLIA** main terminal and the **LCCT**. It departs from Melaka Sentral (RM21.90). Check www.bjaya.com/airport.html for timetables.

Car hire
Avis, 124 Jln Bendahara, T06-284 6710; **Hawk**, T06-283 7878; **Sintat**, Renaissance Melaka Hotel, Jln Bendahara, T06-284 8888; **Thrifty**, G-5 Pasar Pelancong, Jln Tun Sri Lanang, T06-284 9471.

Taxi
Taxi drivers in Melaka refuse to use their meters. Bargain hard. When directing a taxi be careful not to confuse street names with general district areas; use the former whenever possible. There are taxi ranks outside major hotels and shopping centres. From 0100-0600 there is a 50% surcharge.

There is a taxi station at the bus station on Jln Tun Razak. Taxis leave for **KL**, **Seremban**, **Penang**, **Mersing** and **Johor Bahru**. Passengers for Singapore must change taxis at the long-distance terminal in JB.

Johor Bahru p68
Air
MAS, **Firefly** and **AirAsia** fly into Senai, JB's airport, 20 km north of the city. There are shuttle buses every 30 mins between the airport and City Lounge in the Central Bus Terminal, Kotaraya (40 mins, RM8). Taxis also run from JB to Senai. Regular

connections with **KL**, **Subang**, **Kota Bharu**, **Kota Kinabalu**, **Kuching**, **Miri** and **Penang Miri and Sibu**.

Airline offices MAS, Plaza Pelangi, Menara Pelangi, Jln Kuning, Taman Pelangi, T07-334 1003, 2 km from town centre. AirAsia, JOTIC, 2 Jln Ayer Molek, T07-222 4760.

Boat
JB's ferry terminal to the east of the causeway operates ferry services to **Tanjung Belungkor**. Bumboats leave from various points along Johor's coastline for **Singapore**; most go to **Changi Point** (Changi Village), where there is an immigration and customs post. The boats run 0700-1600 and depart when full (12 passengers). There is a passenger ferry from Tanjung Belungkor (JB) to **Changi Ferry Terminal** 3 times a day, T06-5323 6088.

Bus
Local buses and shuttles to Senai Airport leave from the Central BusTerminal on Jln Wong Ah Fook.

There are a number of services running to **Singapore**. Useful buses include Causeway Link CW1 linking Larkin and Kotaraya with **Kranji MRT** (RM1.20) and **SBS 170** from Larkin to Queen Street via Kranji MRT (RM1.90). Passengers need to disembark at both customs posts with all their luggage.

The Larkin Bus Terminal is 4 km north of town and is used by inter-city buses and some local buses. Tickets can be booked at the station itself (slightly cheaper) or from agents opposite the railway station on Jln Tun Abdul Razak. Regular connections with **Melaka** (RM19), **KL** (RM31), **Ipoh** (RM50), **Butterworth** (RM70), **Mersing** (RM10.20), **Kuantan** (RM26.40) and **Kota Bahru** (RM59.20).

Car hire
It is cheaper to hire a car in JB than in Singapore, but check if you are allowed to drive into Singapore. **Avis**, Tropical Inn Hotel, 15 Jln Gereja, T07-224 4824; **Budget**, Suite 216, 2nd floor, Orchid Plaza, T07-224 3951; **Calio**, Tropical Inn, Jln Gereja, T07-223 3325; **Halaju Selatan**, 4M-1 Larkin Complex, Jln Larkin; **Hertz**, Room 646, Puteri Pacific Hotel, Jln Salim, T07-223 7520; **National**, 50-B ground floor Bangunan Felda, Jln Sengget, T07-223 0503; **Sintat**, 2nd floor, KOMTAR, Jln Wong Ah Fook, T07-222 7110; **Thrifty**, Holiday Inn, Jln Dato Sulaiman, T07-333 2313.

Taxi
The main taxi station is attached to the Larkin bus terminal 4 km north of town. Taxis to **KL**, **Melaka**, **Mersing** and **Kuantan**.

Train
The station is on Jln Campbell, near the Causeway, off Jln Tun Abdul Razak. Regular connections with **KL** and destinations on both the east and west coast. Taking the train from JB costs less than half the price of a ticket bought from Singapore. 3 daily departures to **KL** (0912 continues to **Butterworth**, 1418 and 2355). See www.ktmb.com.my.

Pulau Tioman *p68, map p69*
Air
To and from **Singapore** and **Subang** daily. The single fare from Tioman to Subang is around RM230 and to Singapore around RM300. Baggage allowance 10 kg. A bus from the **Berjaya Tioman Resort** meets each arrival and transports guests to the hotel. Alternatively, walk to the pier and catch one of the sea taxis.

Airline offices Berjaya Air operates from Berjaya Resort, T07-419 1309, www.berjaya-air.com.

Boat
Fast boats from **Mersing** to Tioman depart 2-3 times a day depending on the tides (2 hrs, RM35). During the monsoon season (Nov-Feb) departures can be erratic;

boats may not run if there are insufficient passengers and the sea can get quite rough. All boats land on the west coast of Tioman and call at the main kampongs – tell the boatman where you want to disembark.

Beaches and kampongs are connected by a sea taxi service. Prices are usually based on a minimum of 2 people chartering the vessel. Single travellers have to pay the price for 2. Bargain hard. It is necessary to charter a boat to get to the waterfalls (on the south coast) and Kampong Juara. Sea taxi fares (per person) from Kampong Tekek to **Kampong Ayer Batang**, RM20, **Panuba**, RM20, **Salang**, RM40, **Paya**, RM30, **Genting** RM40, **Nipah**, RM60, **Juara**, RM150. The east coast is accessible by taxi, around RM40 per person, by boat or by the jungle trail.

Mersing *p70*
Boat

A RM5 **marine park conservation fee** must be paid before boarding any boat to Tioman and other islands. The payment booth is on the left as you enter the departure point at the jetty.

The jetty is a 15-min walk from the long-distance bus stand. Most of the ticket offices are by the jetty but boat tickets to the islands are also sold from booths near the bus stop. Trips from Mersing can be extremely rough during the monsoon season; boats will sometimes leave Mersing in the late afternoon, at high tide, but rough seas can delay the voyage. It is advisable only to travel during daylight hours. During peak monsoon all ferry services are cancelled.

At present only **Bluewater Express** boats are making the trip over to **Tioman**. The timetable is highly erratic and dependent on the tides. There are 2-3 boats leaving daily, between 0730 and 1630. Tickets cost RM35 (2 hrs) and stop at **Kampong Genting, Berjaya Tioman Beach Resort, Kampong Tekek, Kampong Ayer Batang** and **Kampong Salang**, and you must tell the boat workers where you want to disembark.

Bus

The local bus station is on Jln Sulaiman opposite the Country Hotel.

Long-distance buses leave from 2 locations: those not originating in Mersing leave from the blue bus stand in front of the Timotel (buy a ticket at the bus station first) and those that start from Mersing leave from the new bus station just behind the Timotel (follow the signs from the roundabout). Tickets can be bought from Plaza R&R or from agents in town. Regular connections with **KL** (RM29.80), **Johor Bahru** (RM10.20), **Kuantan** (RM16.30), **Cherating** (RM22), **Terengganu** (RM34), **Ipoh** (change in KL, RM42), **Singapore** (RM25.20) and **Kota Bharu** (RM48.10). Buses heading north to Kuantan and Kuala Terengganu depart between 1100 and 1400. They are often booked out; reserve your ticket a few days in advance.

Taxi

Taxis leave from Jln Sulaiman opposite the Country Hotel, next to the local bus station; **KL, JB** (RM100) (for Singapore, change at JB), **Melaka, Kuala Terengganu** and **Kuantan** (RM100-120).

❶ Directory

Melaka and around *p63, map p64*
Banks Bumiputra, Jln Kota; HSBC, Jln Kota. Several banks on Jln Hang Tuah near bus station and Jln Munshi Abdullah. **Immigration** Bangunan Persekutuan, Jln Hang Tuah, T06-282 4958 (for visa extensions). **Internet** Several; RM3 per hr. **Medical services** Straits Hospital, 37 Jln Parameswara, T06-282 2344. **Police** Jln Kota, T06-282 2222. **Tourist Police**, Jln Kota, T06-285 4114. **Post office** General Post Office, T06-283 3844, off Jln Kota next to Christ Church.

Johor Bahru *p68*
Banks Bumiputra, HSBC and
United Asia are on Bukit Timbalan.
Immigration 1st floor, Block B, Wisma
Persektuan, Jln Air Molek, T07-224 4253.
Internet On Jln Wong Ah Fook. **Medical
services** Sultanah Aminah General
Hospital, Jln Skudai. **Post office**
Jln Tun Dr Ismail.

Mersing *p70*
Banks Maybank, Jln Ismail; UMBC,
Jln Ismail, no exchange on Sat. Money
changer on Jln Abu Bakar and **Giamso
Safari**, 23 Jln Abu Bakar also changes TCs.
Internet Mersing EasyNet Café, Jln
Dato Mohd Ali. **Medical services**
Doctor: Klinik Grace, 48 Jln Abu Bakar,
T07-799 2399. **Post office** Jln Abu Bakar.

East Coast Peninsula

It might just be on the other side of the Peninsula, but Malaysia's east coast could as well be on a different planet than the populous, hectic and industrialized west coast. Its coastline, made up of the states of Johor, Pahang, Terengganu and Kelantan, is lined with coconut palms, dotted with sleepy fishing kampongs and interspersed with rubber and oil palm plantations, paddy fields, beaches and mangroves. The string of islands stretching all along the coast offers a mix of lazy getaways from the acclaimed snorkelling and diving sites to parties and BBQs on the beach. For an insight into Malay traditions and artistry, Kota Bharu in the north stages events from kite flying to drumming sessions, while Kuala Terengganu is a souvenir hunting ground with fine silverware and handicraft markets.

If you plan on visiting any of the beaches or islands on the east coast, and especially if you're hoping to dive, the best time to visit is between February and September to avoid the rainy season. During the winter monsoon (November to February), the seas are very rough and many island resorts are closed and boat operators pack up business. Between May and September is the best time for turtle spotting.

Taman Negara National Park → *For listings, see pages 90-100.*

Taman Negara is Malaysia's largest and most popular national park, with excellent opportunities for trekking and wildlife spotting. Covering 434,000 ha of mountainous jungle, it includes Gunung Tahan, the highest mountain on the Peninsula (2187 m). This area was left untouched by successive ice ages and has been covered in jungle for 130 million years, making it older than the rainforests in the Congo or Amazon basins. Vegetation ranges from riverine species and lowland forest to cloud and moss forest at higher elevations and on to a strange subalpine environment rich in strange pitcher plants close to the summit of Gunung Tahan. More than 250 species of bird have been recorded in Taman Negara, and mammals resident in the park include wild ox (gaur), sambar, barking deer, tapir, civet cat, wild boar and even the occasional tiger and elephant herd. However, the more exotic mammals rarely put in an appearance, especially in areas closer to Kuala Tahan.

Taman Negara

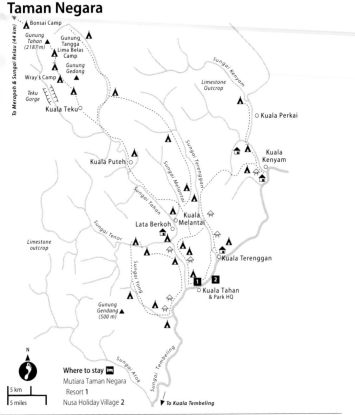

Trekking equipment

A good pair of walking boots is essential even for short excursions, as well as a thick pair of socks and long (loose) trousers. Leeches are common after rain; spraying clothes and boots with insect repellent and wearing leech socks helps. When crossing rivers, hiking sandles or cheap rubber deck shoes help to keep your balance on the slippery rocks. Those undertaking higher altitude treks, such as the Gunung Tahan Trail, will need a good fleece, raingear and a sleeping bag. A good torch is essential for those going to hides, as is a water bottle. A raincover and waterproof bags are useful. Equipment can be hired from the shop at Park HQ.

The park is open year-round but if you intend to visit from October to January, check the weather and river levels in advance. March is the driest month, with 50 mm rainfall.

Visiting Taman Negara National Park

Getting there   Taman Negara is 250 km northeast of KL and can be reached by bus, boat and by train from many different directions. Various companies run tours, but it is quite possible to visit independently. The nearest town is Jerantut; a local bus (RM6) runs two to three times daily to **Park HQ** ① *office open 0800-2200*, in the sleepy riverside village of Kuala Tahan on the south boundary of the park. It is accessible by boat from Kuala Tembeling, a two- to three-hour beautiful journey (or a mundane bus journey). All visitors must check in at reception. The **Department of Wildlife** has a bureau at the Kuala Tembeling jetty and issues permits and licences. You need a permit before entering the park (bring photocopies of your passport). Park permit RM1; fishing licence RM10; camera licence RM5. Those who arrive at Kuala Tembeling jetty without booking may be turned away if boats are full. The website www.tamannegara.org has useful information, including a weekly weather forecast and information on flooding and river levels. ⏩ *See Transport, page 96.*

Staying in the park   There is usually plenty of accommodation for all budgets, but book well in advance for public holidays or in high season. Accommodation can be booked at Kuala Tahan HQ or online at www.tamannegara.org. Fishing lodges (**$$**) have beds and mattresses, but no bedding or cooking equipment is provided. There are chalets in various villages around the park, usually booked up by tour agencies. Visitor lodges for hides at Kuala Terengganu and Kuala Kenyam are away from the crowds but are surprisingly comfortable with attached bathrooms and restaurant.

Hides   It is possible to spend a night in one of the wildlife observation hides, RM5 per night. These are raised up among the trees at Tabang, Belau, Yong, Cegar Anjing and Kumbang and have no facilities other than sleeping space and a pit latrine. Some hides (*bumbun*) are a five-minute walk from Park HQ, while others are a day's trek or boat ride away. You are more likely to see wildlife at the hides further from the Park HQ, as the number of visitors has begun to frighten animals away. Rats, monitor lizards and wild pigs are among the animals not so easily frightened: food bags must be tied up securely at night. During popular periods and on weekends it is best to book your spot. The main breeding time is the dry season (March to September).

Trekking

Trails are signposted from Park HQ; full details on all routes are available. Tours are conducted twice daily by guides and these include night walks and cave treks. Independent day walks can be taken to caves, swimming holes, waterfalls, along rivers (again with swimming areas), to salt-licks and hides and through forest. Longer multi-day treks are also possible but guides must be taken; the most demanding is climbing Gunung Tahan (see below).

Gunung Tahan There are three approaches to climbing the mountain (2187 m), none should be under-estimated, especially during bad weather. A maximum of 48 hikers are allowed on the trail at any one time, so it's best to book in advance. The first route is an eight- to nine-day tough trek from Park HQ at Kuala Tahan. The second route takes seven days, following the same route from Kuala Tahan to the summit before descending the northwest side of the mountain and exiting the park at Sungai Relau. From this point, a park pick-up can be arranged (if booked in advance) and you can be dropped off at the western Park HQ near Merapoh. From Merapoh it's possible to continue your journey by train to the north or south. The third and shortest route (four to five days) involves climbing the peak on a return trek from the Merapoh and the park entrance at Sungai Relau.

Other activities

The **canopy walk** ⓘ *Sat-Thu 1100-1500 and Fri 0900-1200, RM5*, is worth a visit in order to take in jungle life at close proximity. The walkway is suspended about 40 m above the forest floor and stretches for over 530 m making it the world's longest longest canopy walkway. Also popular are fishing and boat trips. ⏵ *See What to do, page 95.*

Jerantut

This is the nearest town to Kuala Tembeling and the most popular entry point into Taman Negara, some 16 km away and RM15 by taxi. For those travelling to the park on public transport it may be necessary to spend a night here and there is a range of accommodation on offer, plus backpacker-friendly tour agencies.

Kenong Rimba National Park → *For listings, see pages 90-100.*

Not far from Taman Negara, Kenong Rimba includes the Kenong River Valley and encompasses some 120 sq km. The park is home to the Batik Orang Asli tribe, who are shifting cultivators. There is a network of Asli trails around the park and several caves and waterfalls. There are two campsites along the river, and chalets. The park is a good alternative to Taman Negara. Though it may not have the same variety of animal life (especially large mammals), it is less touristy and cheaper. A useful website is www.endemicguides.com, which outlines some of the park's climbing, trekking and caving options. Treks from two to four days are possible in Kenong Rimba.

Visiting Kenong Rimba National Park

This park is 1½ hours east of Kuala Lipis by boat down the Jelai River to Kampong Kuala Kenong and is managed by **Kuala Lipis District Forest Office** ⓘ *Government Office Complex, Kuala Lipis, T09-312 1723.* Both a guide and permit are needed before you will be allowed into the park. For tours and treks to Kenong Rimba, see Kuala Lipis What to do, page 96. Entrance to the park is from Batu Sembilan jetty (20 minutes) or an hour's boat ride from the jetty in Kuala Lipis.

The giant leatherback turtle

The giant leatherback turtle is so-called for its leathery carapace (shell). It is the biggest sea turtle and one of the largest reptiles in the world. The largest grow to 3 m in length and can weigh up to 700 kg. They spend most of their lives in the mid-Pacific Ocean and return to Rantau Abang each year to lay their eggs (one of just five main breeding sites in the world). Up to 10,000 turtles used to visit the beach but their numbers are seriously diminishing.

Eggs are poached for their supposed aphrodisiac qualities and the shell is fashioned into combs and cigarette boxes. The Fisheries Department collects up to 50,000 eggs each season for controlled hatching. Once released, many are picked off by predators, such as gulls and fish, and few reach adulthood. Driftnet fishing and pollution add to the problem. As a result, these beautiful creatures are now an endangered species.

Kuala Lipis

Kuala Lipis is a pleasant and relaxed town on the Jelai and Lipis rivers. Unlike most of Malaysia's towns, there has been very little development and many colonial buildings still survive. In the late 19th century it grew to prominence as a gold-mining town and, for a short period, was the area's administrative capital. Today it's a good base from which to trek to Kenong Rimba and is not without charm.

Kampong Cherating and around → *For listings, see pages 90-100.*

A quiet seaside village, set among coconut palms, a short walk from the beach, Kampong Cherating has become a haven for those who want to sample kampong life or just hang out in a simple chalet-style budget resort. Over the years it has become more upmarket. There is a large beach, better for windsurfing than swimming, and a couple of beautiful hidden coves tucked into the rocky headland. It is possible to hire boats to paddle through the mangroves of the Cherating River, to the south side of the kampong, where there is a good variety of birdlife as well as monkeys, monitor lizards and otters. Demonstrations of *silat*, the Malay martial art, can be arranged in the village, as well as top-spinning, kite-flying and batik-printing. In the 1990s the place was a booming resort with a vibrant backpacker scene. However, in more recent times, tourist numbers have dropped considerably and the increasing number of Malaysian visitors has yet to breach the gap. The best beach nearby is **Kemasik**, 28 km north. However, the real highlight of the area is **Rantau Abang** (see below), the nesting site for five different species of turtle.

Arriving in Kampong Cherating

The nearest airport is Kuantan, a 40-minute drive. The bus stop is on the main road 500 m from the kampong itself. There are connections with Singapore, KL and destinations on the east coast. ▸▸ *See Transport, page 97.*

Cherating Travel Post, is a useful first port of call for information and offers travel tickets, car and bike hire, internet and tours.

Rantau Abang

This strung-out beachside settlement owes its existence to turtles. Every year between May and September, five different species of turtle (Penyu in Malay) come to lay their eggs including the endangered giant leatherbacks. During the peak egg-laying season (July-August), the beach gets very crowded. Some areas have restricted access for conservation purposes and a small admission charge is levied. Turtle-watching is free along the stretch around the **Turtle Information Centre** ① *13th Mile Jln Dungun, opposite the big Plaza R&R, T09-844 1533, open Jun-Aug and Sep-Apr*, which has an excellent exhibition and about turtles, focusing on the giant leatherback. The Fisheries Department runs three hatcheries to protect the eggs from predators and egg hunters; these can be visited.

There is a ban on flash photography and unruly behaviour is punishable by a RM1000 fine or six months' imprisonment. Camp fires, excessive noise and littering are illegal. In the 1950s, the annual nesting count stood at around 11,000, a sharp contrast to today's low numbers (1999 had a count of 10 nestings). The dwindling numbers have been blamed on increased fishing activity along the east coast, tourism and higher pollution levels in the sea and along the shoreline.

Kuala Terengganu and around → For listings, see pages 90-100.

The royal capital of Terengganu state was a small fishing port (the state accounts for about a quarter of all Malaysia's fishermen) until oil and gas money started pumping into development projects in the 1980s. The town has long been a centre for arts and crafts, and is known for its *kain songket* (Malay cloth), batik, brass and silverware. The focal point of the town is the central market, **Pasar Besar Kedai Payang** ① *Jln Sultan Zainal Abidin, 0700-1800*, particularly in the early morning, when the fishing fleet comes in. The town's colourful history is revealed in the Chinese shophouses and temple, in the **Zainal Abdin Mosque** ① *Jln Masjid*, and the ceremonial house of **Istana Maziah**, once home to the

Kuala Terengganu

Where to stay 🛌
Awi's Yellow House 1
Ming Star 15
Ping Anchorage 14
Seaview 8
Seri Malaysia 10

Restaurants 🍴
Billi's Kopitiam 1

Terengganu royal family. The **State Museum** ⓘ *5 km southwest of Terengganu in Losong, at the end of Jln Losong Feri, facing Pulau Sekati, daily 0900-1700, RM5, 15 mins by bus, 10 mins by taxi,* is one of the largest in the country. It exhibits rare Islamic porcelain, silver jewellery, musical instruments and weaponry, including a fine selection of *parangs* and *krises*. Around Terengganu numerous kampongs specialize in handicrafts (see Shopping, page 95).

Arriving in Kuala Terengganu

Sultan Mahmud Airport is 18 km northwest of town; a taxi into town costs RM25. There are regular flights from KL as well as Penang, Singapore and Subang (Sumatra). Buses connect with major destinations across the country. There are plenty of local taxis ►► *See Transport, page 97.*

For information contact **Tourism Malaysia** ⓘ *5th floor, Menara Yayasan Islam Terengganu, Jln Sultan Omar, T09-622 1433.* **State Tourist Information Centre (TIC)** ⓘ *77A Jln Sultan Zainal Abidin, near Istana Meziah on the jetty, T09-622 1553, www.tourism. terengganu.gov.my, Sun-Thu 0800-1700, Fri-Sat 0900-1500.* This is an impressive-looking place bursting with information. Also see www.terengganutourism.com.

Marang

ⓘ *From the main road, follow signs to LKIM Komplex from the north end of the bridge.*
This is a colourful Malay fishing kampong at the mouth of the Marang River, although it has been buffeted by the vagaries of the tourist industry over the last couple of decades. Despite development, it is still a lovely village, with its shallow lagoon full of fishing boats. The best beach is opposite Pulau Kapas at Kampong Ru Muda. It was the centre of a mini-gold rush in 1988 when gold was found 6 km up the road at Rusila. On the road north of Marang there are a number of batik workshops, all of which welcome visitors.

Pulau Kapas

Pulau Kapas is 6 km (20 minutes) off the coast, with some good beaches and a very laid-back atmosphere. Those wanting a quiet beach holiday should avoid weekends and public holidays when it is packed. The coral here has been degraded somewhat and there is much better snorkelling at **Pulau Raja**, just off Kapas, which has been declared a marine park. All the guesthouses organize snorkelling and the **Kapas Garden Resort** also has scuba equipment. There is a resort on the privately owned **Pulau Gemia** (Gem Island), just under 1 km from Kapas. Many hotels can also organize a boat trip to the island.

Redang archipelago → *For listings, see pages 90-100.*

The Redang archipelago is a marine park consisting of nine islands 27 km off the coast of Merang. It has some of Malaysia's best reefs, making it one of the most desirable locations for divers. In the months after the monsoon, visibility increases to at least 20 m but during the monsoon the island is usually inaccessible. Line-fishing is permitted and squid fishing, using bright lights, is popular between June and September; the fishermen use a special hook called a *candat sotong*. The lamps light the waters, attracting the squid.

The biggest and best-known island is **Pulau Redang**, but **Pulau Lang Tengah** is also catching up. **Pulau Bidong** was the base for a Vietnamese refugee camp in the 1970s and 1980s and as many as 40,000 were once crammed on this island. The boat people have long gone now, and most of the camp's buildings have rotted away. Agencies in Kuala Terengganu offer day-trips to the island, where there are memorials to the refugees.

and good snorkelling. The only islands with accommodation are Pulau Redang and Pulau Lang Tengah.

Visiting Redang archipelago

Getting there There is a small air strip on Pulau Redang with daily flights from Subang (Sumatra) and Singapore's Budget Terminal. Boats leave from Merang twice daily. Most people travelling to the islands are on all-inclusive package deals. ⏵ *See Transport, page 98.*

Tourist information The independently run website, www.redang.org, offers excellent information and reviews of places and diving on Pulau Redang and Lang Tengah. Tourist information from **Tourism Malaysia** in Kuala Terengganu. Two dives with equipment costs around RM130 on the island, which is fairly reasonable considering the excellent location.

Merang

Merang (not to be confused with Marang) is a small fishing kampong with a long white sandy beach and a number of resort-style places to stay. It is also the departure point for the many offshore islands.

Perhentian Islands → *For listings, see pages 90-100.*

The beautiful Perhentian Islands are just over 20 km off the coast and separated by a narrow sound with a strong current. Despite development in recent years, with more hotels, restaurants, bars, diving outfits and noise, the Perhentians remain a paradise, with excellent diving and snorkelling, magnificent white-sand beaches and some of the best places for swimming on the east coast.

Of the two islands, **Perhentian Besar** (Big Island) is generally more popular with families as it houses slightly more upmarket resorts, although huts on the beach are also available. **Perhentian Kecil** (Small Island) is simpler and attracts a younger crowd of party-going backpackers. There is a fishing village and a turtle hatchery in the middle of **Long Beach** (Pasir Panjang) on Perhentian Kecil. **Note** All visitors must pay a conservation fee of RM5 when visiting the islands.

Visiting the Perhentian Islands

It is important to get to the islands as early in the day as possible due to high demand for accommodation. Boats leave throughout the day from Kuala Besut, which is connected to other towns by regular buses. There are boats between the two islands. ⏵ *See Transport, page 98.*

Kuala Besut

This small fishing village provides a transit link to the Perhentians and has one main place to stay. Business has expanded to cater for those tourists passing through and good food can be found at a series of small restaurants along the waterfront. Kuala Besut has lots of travel agents that sell boat and bus tickets and book accommodation on the island. Taxis, however, seem to favour dropping you off at **Pelangi Travel & Tours**.

Kota Bharu and around → *For listings, see pages 90-100.*

Kota Bharu (KB) is the royal capital of Kelantan, 'the land of lightning', and is situated near the mouth of the Kelantan River. It is one of the country's Malay strongholds, despite its proximity to the Thai border. This was reinforced during the latest general elections when the opposition PAS (Malaysia's Islamic Party) once again managed to secure KB and Kelantan (the only PAS state in the country). The noticeable presence of Jawi (Malay written using Arabic script) and the ceasing of activities during prayer times (Azan) will probably be the most noticeable of the Islamic influences to the visitor. While some people react against the state government's support for an Islamic interpretation of public (and private) morals, Kota Bharu is one of Malaysia's more culturally interesting and colourful towns with eclectic museums, mosques, grandiose royal palaces, an unmissable wet market and an impressive cultural zone.

Kota Bharu

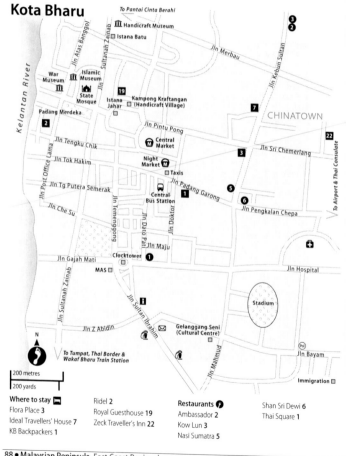

Where to stay 🛏
Flora Place 3
Ideal Travellers' House 7
KB Backpackers 1

Ridel 2
Royal Guesthouse 19
Zeck Traveller's Inn 22

Restaurants 🍴
Ambassador 2
Kow Lun 3
Nasi Sumatra 5

Shan Sri Dewi 6
Thai Square 1

Kelantan is also renowned for its crafts – silverware, weaving and metalworking were partly the result of the state's close relations with the Siamese kingdom of Ayutthaya in the 17th century. The *makyung*, a traditional Malay court dance, is still performed in Kelantan and *wayang kulit* (shadow puppet plays) still provide entertainment on special occasions.

Arriving in Kota Bharu

Getting there and around KB's airport is 8 km from town; a taxi costs RM25. There are frequent connections with KL, Penang and Subang (Sumatra). The train station is 6 km out of town at Wakaf Bharu. The line runs south to KL and Singapore. There are three bus terminals but most express buses depart from the most central. Buses run to most towns, including to Rantau Panjang and Pengkalan Kubor on the Thai border. Taxis have replaced trishaws as the most popular form of local transport. There is also a city bus service. ▸▸ *See Transport, page 99.*

Tourist information The **Tourist Information Centre** ① *Jln Sultan Ibrahim, T09-748 5534, Sat-Thu 0800-1300 and 1400-1700,* is helpful and has a good map of the town. It will arrange taxis and ferries to the islands, as well as booking accommodation on them.

Safety Tourists travelling to Thailand need to be aware that, since 2004, southern Thailand has been plagued by separatist violence that has killed more than 2500 people. The most severely affected Thai states are Narathiwat (adjoins Kelantan), Patani, Songkhla and Yala. Check www.fco.gov.uk for the latest information.

Places in Kota Bharu

The heart of Kota Bharu is the **central market** ① *off Jln Temenggong, daily 0900-2000,* which is one of the most vibrant wet markets in the country. It is housed in an octagonal concrete complex painted green with a glass roof. Nearby is the **Istana Jahar** ① *T09-444 666, Sat-Thu 0830-1645, RM3,* constructed in 1889 by Sultan Mohammed IV and now the 'centre for royal customs'. It exemplifies the skilled craftsmanship of the Kelantanese woodcarvers in its intricately carved beams and panels. The **Kampong Kraftangan (Handicraft Village)** aims to give visitors a taste of Kelantan's arts and crafts all under one roof. The large enclosure, in which merbuk birds (doves) sing in their bamboo cages, contains four wooden buildings built in traditional Malay style. The **Muzium Kraftangan (Handicraft Museum)** ① *Sat-Thu 0830-1645, RM1,* contains traditional Kelantanese crafts and customs. There is also a batik workshop. Opposite, is the **Istana Batu,** the sky-blue Stone Palace, which was built in 1939 and was one of the first concrete buildings in the state and contains many royal possessions.

A little north of the commercial centre is a magnificent two-storey green-and-white mansion with traditional Islamic latticework carving on eaves, which houses the **Islamic Museum** ① *Jln Merdeka, Sat-Thu 1030-1645, donation.* The building is more noteworthy than its contents. Next door, the **War Museum** ① *0830-1645, RM2,* offers an informative account of the Second World War in Southeast Asia. Beginning with Pearl Harbor, it tells the story of the Japanese invasion of Kelantan in 1941 and the subsequent conquest of Malaya.

The **Gelanggang Seni** ① *Jln Mahmud, opposite stadium,* is rather touristy but a good place to see cultural demonstrations. These include: *silat* (Malay self-defence); Kelantan drums, made from hollowed-out logs; top-spinning; *wayang kulit* (shadow-puppets); and kite-flying with the famous paper-and-bamboo *wau bulan* (or Kelantan moon-kites). The latter has been a Kelantanese sport for centuries; the aim is to fly your kite the highest and to defend it by being as aggressive as possible towards other competitors' kites. Kite-flying was a favourite hobby in the heyday of the Melaka sultanate in the 15th century.

East Coast Peninsula listings

For hotel and restaurant price codes and other relevant information, see pages 9-11.

⊖ Where to stay

Taman Negara National Park
p81, map p81

$$$$-$ Mutiara Taman Negara Resort, Kampong Kuala Tahan, T09-266 2200, www.mutiarahotels.com. Book in advance. From 8-bed dorms to chalets and bungalows, some self-catering. Options for visiting Orang Asli settlements, dusk in an observation hide and fishing trips. Also runs a lodge in Kuala Terengganu with chalets and a restaurant.

$$ Teresek Hill View, T09-266 3065. Dorms, basic chalets and more sophisticated bungalows with attached bathrooms.

$$-$ Nusa Holiday Village, 15 mins upriver from Park HQ, T09-266 2369, www.tamannegara-nusaholiday.com. my. Dorms, comfortable Malay houses, cottages and simple A-frame huts. The more expensive rooms have hot water and well-netted windows. Restaurant. Trips organized. Take a longboat from Park HQ (shuttle boat every 2 hrs); direct daily service from Kuala Tembeling at 0900 and 1400 (Fri 1430), RM70.

Camping

Mutiara Taman Negara Resort, see opposite, has facilities (RM1) and rents out tents, as do tourist agencies at Kuala Tahan. Check the quality before setting out. See map, page 81, for camping locations.

Jerantut *p83*

$$ Wau Hotel and Café, K1, Pusat Perniagaan Sungai Jan, Jalan Sungai Jan, T09-260 2255, www.wauhotels.com. This good-value, mid-priced place has comfy a/c rooms with LCD TV and Wi-Fi. Recommended.

$$-$ Sri Emas, T09-266 4499. Busy little guesthouse with a/c and fan rooms. Fairly clean but the shared bathrooms are a little grotty. Offers excellent information, free transport from bus/train station. Trips organized to the park, dorms, luggage store internet in lobby, restaurant.

$ Jerantut Guesthouse, T09-266 6200. Some rooms have a/c and bathroom, restaurant, popular, daily trips to the park.

Kuala Lipis *p84*

$ Gin Loke, 64 Jln Besar, T09-312 1388. Simple rooms, shared facilities, treks in Kenong Rimba.

$ Kuala Lipis (aka Appu's Guesthouse), 63 Jln Besar, T09-312 3142. Near train station. Dorms and doubles. Some a/c, shared bathrooms, excellent tours and information

$ Persona Rimba Resort Kenong, Kuala Lipis, T09-312 5032. Simple huts. Tours organized.

Kampong Cherating *p84*

$$ Tanjung Inn, turn right at bottom of lane down from main road, after Coconut Inn, T09-581 9081, tanjunginn@jaring.my. The best mid-range spot to stay in Cherating with simple chalets on stilts, some built over a small lake in extensive and gardens. This friendly family-run option also has a number of larger bungalows close to the beach. A charming place to stay. Recommended.

$$-$ The Shadow of the Moon at Half Past Four, T09-581 9086 (the northernmost chalet resort on the loop off the main road). This place has fallen from grace a little in recent times, having changed ownership. Nevertheless, the spooky name sums up the bewitching ambience at this quiet place with simple, rustic cottages set on a forested hillside, with fan and attached bathroom. It offers much more tranquil surroundings than resorts along the beach. Recommended.

$ Matahari Chalets, on the southernmost lane from main road. Attractive bungalows with spacious veranda, some with fridge.
$ Payung Guesthouse, next to the river, and a 2-min walk from the main junction, T019-917 1934. Simple chalets on stilts with attached bathroom. There's a reiki shed with classes offered by David, the owner. There's excellent dining options nearby.

Rantau Abang p84
$$-$ Ismail's, T09-844 1054. Beachside set-up.
$ Dahimah's, 1 km south of visitor centre, T09-845 2483. Restaurant, clean rooms in Malay wooden chalets. Some a/c.

Kuala Terengganu p85, map p85
Cheaper hotels are mainly at the jetty end of Jln Sultan Ismail and on Jln Banggol.
$$ Hotel Ming Star, 217 Jln Sultan Zainal Abidin, T09-622 866, www.mingstarhotel.com. New hotel with small, but well-designed modern a/c rooms with attached bathroom, cable TV and Wi-Fi access. This is the best option in town at this price range, but is somewhat hampered by its location, which is a fair stroll from the centre.
$$ Seaview, 18a Jln Masjid Abidin, T09-622 1911, sv_hotel@yahoo.com. While the paint might be peeling in some of the rooms, this place is not bad value. Rooms have Wi-Fi access, a/c, cable TV and attached bathroom with hot water. Rooms at the front have good views of the *istana*.
$$ Seri Malaysia, Lot 1640, Jln Hiliran, T03-2161 8223, www.serimalaysia.com.my. A/c, good restaurant, well run, TV, minibar, light airy rooms overlooking the river.
$ Awi's Yellow House, Pulau Duyung Besar, T09-624 5046, rohanilongvet@hotmail.com. Built on stilts over the river, very popular. Dorm and *atap*-roofed huts, some with balconies, pleasant with cool breezes, kitchen. Take a boat from Jln Bandar, or a taxi from KT via the new Sultan Mahmud bridge.
$ Ping Anchorage, 77A Jln Sultan Sulaiman, T09-626 2020, www.pinganchorage.com.

my. The most popular backpackers' haunt in town with clued-up management offering excellent local information and tours of the city and beyond. Offers functional, somewhat unexciting rooms, 3 of which have a/c and attached bathroom. There are fan rooms (shared bathroom) and a dorm (RM8). Wi-Fi is available in the rooms nearest the road. The rooftop café here is a great place to mingle and have a beer.

Marang p86
Also some hotels at Kampong Rhu Muda, 2 km before the bridge over the Marang River.
$$-$ Angullia Beach House, 12¼ milestone, Kampong Rhu Muda, T09-618 1322, www.angulliaresort.com. Extremely friendly family-run chalet resort on lovely sheltered stretch of beach with excellent sunset views. Very clean chalets, some a/c. Leafy, well-kept grounds with play area for children. Good set meals. Wi-Fi available.
$ Green Mango Inn, A-71 Bandar Marang, T019-946 9409. Fan, basic A-frame chalets or doubles. Excellent atmosphere, good views, small garden and sitting area with games.
$ Mare Nostrum Holiday Resort, Kampong Rhu Muda, T09-618 2417. A/c, restaurant, clean and hospitable, boat trips, pleasant, well-kept compound with chalets.

Pulau Kapas p86
$$$-$$ Duta Puri, T09-624 6090, www.dutaresorts.com. The most upmarket place to stay. Charming chalets. All rooms have TV, minibar and wooden floors.
$ The Lighthouse, T019-215 3558. Owner Din is a real character. The best budget option. All rooms are in an atmospheric longhouse. Very mellow. Lots of beach games, BBQs and the **Tropical Hut** bar.

Redang archipelago p86
Resorts on Redang offer competitive package deals – check with **Tourism**

Malaysia in Kuala Terengganu (see page 86). A typical 2-day/2-night trip costs RM300 per person including food, camping and snorkelling equipment.

Merang *p87*

$ Kembara Resort, 474 Pantai Peranginan Merang, 21010 Setiu, T09-623 8771. On a beautiful palm-fringed beach south of the jetty, garden, 8 bungalows and rooms with bathroom and fan. Dorms. Kitchen.
$ Stingray Beach Chalet, T019-327 8855. Right on the beach, fan, bathroom, immaculately run and offers a dive service.

Perhentian Islands *p87*
Perhentian Besar

The majority of accommodation is on the west coast or in the secluded bay of Telok Dalam.
$$$ Tuna Bay Island Resort, T09-697 9779, www.tunabay.com.my. Pretty wooden chalets and a lovely open-air restaurant serving excellent fresh seafood. Dive centre and travel agency. Excellent packages if booked through their website. Wi-Fi available.
$$$-$ Flora Bay Chalet, Telok Dalam, T09-691 1666, www.florabayresort.com. Comfortable chalets and swanky A-frames, all rooms here have private bathroom and 24-hr elecricity. More expensive rooms have hot water and mini-fridge. The hotel has its own PADI 5-star dive centre (www.florabaydivers.com).
$$ Mama's, T019-984 0232, www.mamas chalet.com. Fan, shower. Selection of simple chalets mainly used by families or couples. There's excellent snorkelling offshore and we frequently receive reports of shark and turtle sightings a quick swim from the shore. A-frames here are good value. Recommended.
$$ New Coco Hut Chalets, T09-697 7988. Comfortable A-frame huts with private bathroom. More expensive huts have TV and mini-fridge. It's worth splashing out a little more for a sea-view room as the

garden huts, though good value, are squashed together.
$$ Perhentian Watercolours Resort, T017-938 0952, www.watercoloursworld. com. Brightly coloured fan rooms (some a/c in the sea-view rooms) near a lovely bit of beach. The restaurant here is renowned for seafood and pizza (although it can take some time coming). Diving, snorkelling and kayaking offered. Internet available.
$$-$ Abdul's, T09-697 7058. Decent chalets on the beach, fan and shower, with popular restaurant. Good local reputation.

Perhentian Kecil

There is more budget accommodation on Kecil although the arrival of the red-roofed concrete **Bubu** resort, which has angered guesthouse operators, has made a stab at making the island more upmarket. Accommodation is split, with some huts on the beautiful white sandy beach of Pasir Panjang (Long Beach), on the east side of the island, and some on Coral Bay, on the west. Those looking to party head to Long Beach, which has a good range of eateries and a younger crowd. Coral Bay is much smaller and can feel a bit crowded with its densely packed accommodation. The coral in Coral Bay is mostly dead, but the sea here is clear and offers pleasant swimming. The 2 are separated by a 10-min walk through the forest – easy by day but not so simple at night! There are a couple of places at the southern tip, not far from Perhentian village and an isolated spot at Teluk Kerma.
$$$ Shari La Resort, Coral Bay, T09-6911 500, www.shari-la.com. New, upmarket place with 74 spacious colourful a/c rooms with attached bathroom with hot water, and some with excellent sea views. The resort takes up a sizeable portion of the promontory at the north end of Coral Bay, and its restaurant is guilty of blaring Bob Marley music which shatters the calm. Internet available. Excellent promotional rates.
$$ Maya Beach Resort, Coral Bay, T019-924 1644. Extremely popular operation

that constantly has to refuse people due to being full. Trails of disappointed tourists can be seen lugging their gear back along the beach in the hunt for somewhere else to stay. The 12 fan chalets here are nicely decorated, simple and set in spacious grounds that offer more privacy than most. Excellent little café, internet access and very friendly staff. Internet available. Recommended.

$$ Mohsin, T014-548 7863. Accommodation is in rows of blue-roofed huts on a hill, all with excellent views of Long Beach. Rooms are simple, yet modern and have attached bathroom with hot water. Cheerful owner with bizarre pricing system. Make sure to negotiate for your room; the longer you stay, the larger the discount.

$$ Senja Bay, T09-691 1799, www.senja bay.com. Recently refurbished resort, which is equally as popular as the **Maya**. Chalets and A-frames here are comfortable and have hot water, and some are lined along the beach with glorious sea views. The elevated restaurant serves fairly average Western food, but has sublime views, free Wi-Fi access for guests and the cheapest internet access on the island for non-guests.

$$-$ Bintang View, up the hill on the way to Coral Bay from Long Beach, T013-997 1563. Owned by an Irish lady, Finola, and her local husband Joe, this is a newcomer to the scene. It's refreshingly located far enough away from the beach to be away from any cloying scene, and close enough to be in the sea in 5 mins. The chalets are a mixture of old and new, all with fan, veranda with views and mosquito net. Bathroom facilities are shared, but kept spotless. The restaurant here also serves some fine pasta dishes and salads. Recommended.

Kota Bharu p88, map p88
Plenty of budget options and homestays.
$$$ Flora Place, 202 Jln Kebun Sultan, T09-7477 888, www.thefloraplace.com. Smart hotel mainly used by people in

transit to the Perhentians. Rooms are not huge, but are smart and clean with a/c, fridge, cable TV and firm mattresses. They have a hotel on the Perhentians and can arrange transfers and package deals. There's a diving equipment shop on the ground floor. Wi-Fi in lobby.

$$$-$$ Ridel Hotel, Block A, Pelangi Mall, Jln Pasar Lama, T09-747 7000, www. ridelhotel.com.my. Large new block erected on the riverside, giving some rooms superb views. The a/c rooms are spotless, ultra-modern and have cable TV, Wi-Fi access, smart bathrooms and a choice of town or river view. Guests can even choose from 4 different colour schemes. Recommended.

$$$-$$ Royal Guesthouse, Jln Hilir Kota, T09-743 0008, royalgh@streamyx.com. Excellent-value accommodation in the cultural heart of the city, with a selection of comfortable a/c rooms with TV and hot-water bathroom. This is a modern and stylish hotel, and features one of the city's best restaurants.

$$ Ideal Travellers' House, 5504a Jln Padang Garong, T09-744 2246, www.ugo ideal.com. Quiet family-run option, with rooms echoing to the sound of bird song, pleasantly located away from the busy city streets. The hotel badly needs some investment as mattresses are squashy, bathrooms are clean but with chipped toilet bowl and broken flush and walls are grubby. Can help with onward travel arrangements. Wi-Fi available.

$$-$ KB Backpackers Lodge, 1872 Jln Padang Garong, T09-748 8841, www.kb-backpackers.com.my/lodge.html. Popular hostel in the city centre with a selection of clean and functional a/c and fan rooms, some with no natural light. There is a rooftop terrace with a small bar serving beer and internet available in the lobby. Dorms available (RM10).

$$-$ Zeck's Traveller's Inn, 7088 Jln Sri Cemerlang, T09-743 1613, zecktravellers@ yahoo.com It's a bit of a hike into town, but this place is peaceful and comfortable and offers the budget traveller the best value for money. Rooms are well kept and bright, mostly fan and shared bathroom, but there is 1 a/c room with attached bathroom with hot shower. Wi-Fi available. Friendly owner. Dorm (RM10). Recommended.

🍴 Restaurants

Kampong Cherating *p84*
$$ Cherating Lagoon Seafood Restaurant, (next to **Cherating Palm Resort**). Open 1100-0200. Chinese dishes, seafood and some Western food, this place has the cheapest beers in town – look for the RM5 bottles of Malaysian beer, Jaz. Gets busy at the weekend.
$ Payung Café, next to the **Payung Guesthouse**. Open 0800-1100, 1700-2400. Run by a friendly local family, this cheery place offers Wi-Fi, big-screen TV and ice-cold beers to accompany its menu of good pizza and pasta. This is also the place to go for a breakfast of omelettes and juice.
$ Restoran Duyong, inside the **Duyong Beach Resort**, T09-581 9578. Lovely setting on raised wooden terrace at edge of beach, lobster and prawns sold by weight.
$ Surf and Chill Café, T017-267 9969. Open 1800-2400. Owned by young entrepreneur Nasz, this small bar/eatery offers the finest cheeseburgers on the east coast, as well as beers and a pool table. Recommended.

Kuala Terengganu *p85, map p85*
Nasi dagang (trader's rice) is a local speciality of glutinous rice, served with *gulai ikan tongkol* (tuna with tamarind and coconut gravy).
$ Billi's Kopitiam, Jln Dato Isaac. Open 0800-2000. Owned by renowned local gourmand Billi, this little jewel of a place serves up a stunning array of local and fusion dishes. Billi will gladly give recommendations. Things to look out for are the delicious lemongrass infused chicken rendang and the celebrated *nasi lemak goreng*. Highly recommended.

$ Ping Anchorage Travellers' Café, Jln Sultan Sulaiman. Friendly travellers' café on an antique festooned rooftop with views of a leafy kampong to one side and the sea on the other. Dishes are simple Western and Asian and can be washed down with a beer. Good breakfasts. Large TV, used to show football at the weekend. Recommended.

Foodstalls
Gerai Makanan (foodstalls) opposite the bus station, Malay. **Jalan Batu Buruk**, near the Cultural Centre, excellent Malay food and seafood, recommended. **Kampong Tiong** (off Jln Bandar), excellent hawker centre with Malay and Indian food, 0800-late.

Perhentian Islands *p87*
Most chalets have attached restaurants, particularly popular are **Coral View Island Resort**, **New Coco Hut Chalets** and **Tuna Bay**. On Long Beach, **Panorama's** is particularly good. There are 3 almost identical cafés midway down the beach, **Daniel's**, **Family Café**, and **Meeting Point** (all **$**) serving up generic backpacker-friendly fare. At Coral Bay, the 2 busiest eateries are **Amelia's** and **Mama's** (both **$**), with some good local dishes and nightly seafood BBQs.

Kota Bharu *p88, map p88*
Alcohol is only available in certain Chinese coffee shops, notably along Jln Kebun Sultan.
   The Kelantan speciality is *ayam percik* (roast chicken, marinated in spices and served with a coconut-milk gravy). *Nasi tumpang* (banana-leaf funnel of rice layers with prawn and fish curries and salad) is a typical breakfast. Other dishes worth keeping an eye open for include *nasi dagang* (a version of *nasi lemak* with brown rice steeped in coconut milk and served with pickles and fish curry) and *ketupat sotong* (an unusual dish of cuttlefish stuffed with glutinous rice and coated in brown sugar).

\$\$ Ambassador, 7003 Jln Kebun Sultan. Big Chinese coffee shop, Chinese dishes including pork satay, beer available.
\$\$ Kow Lun, 7005 and 7006 Jln Kebun Sultan. Good lively Chinese coffee shop.
\$\$ Malaysia, 2527 Jln Kebun Sultan. Chinese cuisine, speciality steamboat.
\$ Nasi Sumatra, 2527 Jln Kebun Sultan. Open for lunch and early dinner. Indonesian-style curries including *ikan gulai*, *rendang* and some good *percedel* make this a good lunch spot. There are a couple of branches in town. Look for signs saying the food was prepared by Haji Ismail. Recommended.
\$ Shan Sri Dewi, 4213 Jln Kebun Sultan. Popular Indian place with the usual offerings. The *dosai* here, though small, are delcious. The curries can be watery and lack zing.
\$ Thai Square, below Ansar Hotel, Jln Dato Pa. Cheap and authentic Thai food that needs to be eaten quickly to avoid the intoxicating traffic fumes from the busy thoroughfare.

O Shopping

Kuala Terengganu *p85, map p85*
Batik Some of the best batik in Malaysia can be found in the Central Market (Pasar Besar Kedai Payang). There are a number of small craft and batik factories in Kampong Ladang, the area around Jln Sultan Zainal Abidin.

Handicrafts The Central Market is touristy, but offers a range of textiles and brassware. Surrounding kampongs practise silverwork, batik printing, *songket* weaving and *wau* kite building. 7 km south of Kuala Terengganu are the excellent Cendering handicraft centres (take Marang-bound buses from Jln Syed Hussin). Worth visiting are: **Kraftangan Malaysia**, **Nor Arfa Batik Factory**, and the **Sutera Semai** silk factory.

Marang *p86*
Handicrafts The market in Marang has a craft market upstairs and there are several handicraft shops along the main street.
Balai Ukiran Terengganu (Terengganu Wood Carving Centre), Kampong Rhu Rendang, near Marang, master-carver Abdul Malek Ariffin runs the east coast's best-known woodcarving workshop, making a wide range of carved furniture from cengal wood, carved with traditional floral geometric and Islamic calligraphic patterns. Shipping arranged.

Kota Bharu *p88, map p88*
Batik Astaka Fesyer, 782K (3rd floor), recommended; Bazaar Buluh Kubu (Bamboo Fort Bazaar), Jln Tengku Petra Semerak, across the road from Central Market, has scores of batik boutiques.
Handicrafts The Central Market is cheapest. There are numerous handicraft stalls, silver-workers, kite-makers and woodcarvers along the road north to Pantai Cinta Berahi. At Kampong Penambang, on this road, just outside KB, there is a batik and *songket* centre.
Silverware On Jln Sultanah Zainab (near the bridge across the Kelantan River), before junction with Jln Hamzah, there are shops selling Kelantan silver, including **KB Permai**. The **Kampong Kraftangan** (handicraft village) contains a huge range of batik sarongs and ready-mades, silverware, *songket*, basketry and various Kelantanese knick-knacks.

O What to do

Taman Negara National Park
p81, map p81
Boat trips
From Park HQ to the Lata Berkoh rapids on Sungai Tahan, RM120 for 4 people. An enchanting way to see the park.

Fishing

The best months are Feb-Mar and Jul-Aug. There are game fishing lodges at Kuala Terengganu and Kuala Kenyam. The rivers Tahan, Kenyam and the more remote Sepia (tributaries of the Tembeling) are reckoned to be the best waters. There are more than 200 species of fish including the *kelasa* – a renowned sport fish. A permit costs RM10, rods are available for hire.

Tour operators

See also Jerantut, below. **Mutiara Taman Negara Resort**, see page 90, is the park's only luxury resort. 3 days, 2 nights for RM400 including 2 treks. Also runs a shuttle from KL to Kuala Temberling jetty.

Jerantut *p83*

Han Travel, 1A Bandar Baru, Kuala Tembeling, T09-266 2899, www.taman-negara.com. Boat and bus transfers from KL, Kota Bharu and the Cameron Highlands and into the park, hotel bookings plus tour packages. Fairly standard prices and saves a lot of hassle. **NKS Hotel & Travel**, Hotel Sri Emas, T09-260 1777, www.taman-negara-nks.com. Aimed at budget travellers. Bus and boat transfers, package tours, 4 days, 3 nights for RM380. Tours include boat trips, camping, trekking, stay at Orang Asli village and cave exploring.

Kuala Lipis *p84*

Mr Appu Annandaraja of **Kuala Lipis Hotel** runs highly recommended 4-day treks in and out of Kenong Rimba. Trips are also run by: **Gin Loke Hotel**, 64 Jln Besar; and **Tuah Travel & Tours**, 12 Jln Lipis, T09-312144.

Kuala Terengganu *p85, map p85*

Ping Anchorage Travel & Tours, 77A Jln Sultan Sulaiman, T09-626 2020, www.pinganchorage.com.my. Well-organized and efficient, offering seemingly everything. **Turtleliner**, Jln Sultan Masjid Abidin, T09-623 7000. Services include flight booking and confirmation, tours. Helpful staff.

Marang *p86*

MGH (Marang Guest House), T09-618 1976, www.marangguesthouse.com, office by the small jetty, daily 0900-1700. Runs fishing, snorkelling and jungle trips and half-day river tours. Also has chalets (**$$$-$$**) and sells tickets for boats to Pulau Kapas.

Pulau Kapas *p86*

The resorts run diving, snorkelling and fishing trips, and kayaks can be hired. Several companies run boats (fast boat, RM25 return, 20 mins, 0930-1700).

Perhentian Islands *p87*

Most guesthouses arrange snorkelling trips and rent equipment. RM35-40 for a half day, RM15 to hire gear on the beach. Dive shops (PADI) on both islands run courses for all levels. **Turtle Bay Divers** and **Spice Divers** on Kecil are recommended. If snorkelling off Long Beach, head for the patch near Moonlight.

Kota Bharu *p88, map p88*

Kelantan State Tourist Information Centre organizes river and jungle-safari trips. Also organizes 3-day 'Kampong Experience' tours with full board and lodging provided by host families (such as potters, fishermen, batik-makers, kite-makers, silversmiths, top-makers and shadow puppet-makers), for RM285 (all in); minimum 2 people. It also runs short Kelantanese cooking courses.

⊖ Transport

Taman Negara National Park
p81, map p81
Bus and boat

Most visitors get a bus or taxi to **Kuala Tembeling** jetty via Jerantut. There are regular connections from **KL**. Guesthouses and tour operators in KL arrange tickets. **NK** Travel (T03-2072 0336) shuttle bus leaves from outside the Mandarin Pacific Hotel in KL's Chinatown (0830, 3 hrs, RM75 one way including boat ticket). Those staying in the

Bukit Bintang area are able to catch the **Ping Anchorage** (T03-4280 8030) daily shuttle from the Mutiara Hotel at 0900 (RM40). Buses connect with a boat to the park. If you want to take a public bus, departures are from Pekeling bus station in **KL** (access via Titiwangsa LRT and Monorail station). You will need to catch the first bus to make the boat connection to the park in time, or you will have to stay in Jerantut overnight.

At Kuala Tembeling there are boats to the Park HQ at **Kuala Tahan**, 2½ hrs, RM25 one-way. Boats leave at 1400. **Mutiara Resort** has a boat departing at 1300, RM28.

Nusa Holiday Village also operates a boat service from Kuala Tembeling to their own resort departing daily at 0900 and 1400 (Fri 1430), RM70 return.

It is now possible to go by road all the way to Kuala Tahan from **Jerantut**. A public bus runs around 4 times a day to and from Jerantut bus station (0530, 0830, 1315, 1730), RM6, one-way, 1½ hrs.

Jerantut *p83*
Bus/taxi
The bus and taxi station is in town centre. Regular connections from **KL**'s Pekeling terminal (RM13), the first bus departs at 0830. Contact **Perwira Ekspress**, T09-266 3919. Taxis direct to Jerantut from KL leave from the Puduraya bus terminal. From the east coast, there 3 daily buses from **Kuantan** (0830, 1300 and 1500); also taxis.

Kuala Lipis *p84*
Bus
Buses to **KL** Pekeling bus terminal every 1½ hrs, 0830-2030 (2 hrs, RM14.50). Daily connections with **Kota Bharu** and **Kuantan** (3hrs, RM25.80).

Train
There is 1 daily train to Kuala Lipis from **KL** at 2030. From **Singapore** there are 3 daily trains departing at 0430, 1800 and 0715. From **Kota Bharu** (from Wakaf Bharu station, 6 km outside) there are trains at

0718, 1904, 2049, 0408, 1010 and 1530. There are connections with **Jerantut**.

Kampong Cherating *p84*
Air
Sultan Ahmad Shah, Kuantan's airport is 45 mins' drive away. Regular connections with **KL** (MAS only) and **Penang** and **Singapore** with Firefly.

Bus
Regular buses from **Kuantan** (Kemaman bus). Bus stops are on the main road outside the village. Buses to **Rantau Abang**, **Kuala Terengganu**, **Marang**, **Kota Bharu** and as far north as the Thai border at **Rantau Panjang**. For destinations to the south, it is first necessary to go to Kuantan. **Travelpost** can book tickets.

Kuala Terengganu *p85, map p85*
Air
Sultan Mahmud Airport lies 18 km northwest of town, T09-666 4204. Regular connections with **KL**. **Firefly** connects the city with **Singapore**, **Subang** and **Penang** and MAS and AirAsia have daily flights to **KLIA** and **LCCT**.

Airline offices MAS and Firefly, 13 Jln Sultan Omar, T09-622 1415.

Bus
Kuala Terengganu's bus station is just off Jln Tok Lam. Connections to **KL** (3 hrs, RM40), **JB** (9 hrs, RM44), **Kota Bharu** (RM14.20), **Kuantan** (RM17.80), **Rantau Abang** (RM17), **Mersing** (RM34), **Singapore** (RM 59), **Melaka** (RM43), **Butterworth** (RM41, 9 hrs)

Local buses leave from the same station with connections to **Merang**, **Marang** and **Kuala Besut**. For the **Perhentian Islands**, board a bus to Kuala Besut, which goes directly to the jetty. The bus leaves 6 times a day, the most useful departures for travellers leave at 0700, 1000 and 1130 (2½ hrs, RM10.70). After these times, you will have trouble connecting with a boat.

Taxi

Next to the bus station on Jln Masjid and from the waterfront. Destinations include **Kota Bharu**, **Rantau Abang**, **Marang**, **Kuantan**, **KL**, **JB** and **Penang**. Taxi, T09-621 581.

Marang *p86*
Bus

Bus stop on the main road up the hill. Tickets bought from the kiosk on Jln Tg Sulong Musa (sometimes closed so book in advance). Buses to **Kuala Terengganu** every 90 mins. If stuck without a ticket go to the express bus station (taxi RM18). Taxis wait by the jetty.

Redang archipelago *p86*
Air

There is a small air strip on Pulau Redang operated by **Berjaya Air**, www.berjaya-air.com, which flies a 48-seater Dash 7 from **Subang** and **Singapore**'s Budget Terminal. Departure times vary, check website. A one-way flight to Subang/Singapore costs around RM260/RM350 including tax and insurance.

Boat

From **Merang** or the jetty in **Kuala Terangganu** (Berjaya customers only, 2 departures, at 1030 and 1500). It is possible to charter private boats from Merang, RM40 per person one-way. Package deals include transport, see www.redang.org.

Merang *p87*
Bus

2 buses a day to/from **Kuala Terengganu** (RM3). Minibus connections with **Kuala Terengganu**, from Jln Masjid.

Taxi

A/c taxi to **Kuala Terengganu** RM40.

Perhentian Islands *p87*
Boat

Speed boats leave at irregular hours. Tickets are booked through travel agents in Kuala Besut. More boats leave in the morning, so the earlier you can get there the better. Fast boats (RM70 return) leave **Kuala Besut** generally every hour from 0700-1600 (at peak periods), 30 mins, boats carry 8-14 people. These small boats drive very fast and the ride can get bumpy, try to sit at the back near the driver. The ride is exhilarating, and you are required to wear a lifejacket. The same boats leave **Pulau Perhentian** for **Kuala Besut** at 0800, 1200 and occasionally at 1600. Ask a day in advance about the 1600 sailing. Boats cannot land at the beach. Some resort areas have jetties, but for others, you'll have to transfer yourself and your luggage to a tiny 13-ft boat (RM2) for a short scoot to the sands. Those staying at the more remote Pasir Petani Resort on **Perhentian Kecil** should pre-arrange a pick-up time. Travellers should be wary of risking the boat trip too close to the beginning or end of the Dec-Feb monsoon season. If you want to travel between the islands once you are there you will have to hire a water taxi. These motorized dinghies have fixed rates, ask at the guesthouse. A single trip between Long Beach and the opposite beach is RM12.

Bus

There are fairly frequent connections on local buses from the bus station near the jetty to **Kota Bahru** (1½ hrs, RM6) and **Kuala Terrenganu** (2½ hrs, RM10.70). To **Kuala Lumpur**: Mahligia Express bus company, T09-690 3699, leaves twice a day, at around 0830 and at 2030. Buses from KL leave around a similar time. Buses from **Singapore** or **JB** to **Kota Bahru** can drop travellers of at **Jerteh**, where there are frequent local bus connections with **Kuala Besut**.

Taxi

Kuala Terengganu (RM90); Merang Jetty (RM60, for Redang), Kota Bharu (RM50). Taxis from Pasir Puteh or Jerteh to Kuala Besut (RM15).

Kota Bharu p88, map p88

Air

The airport is 8 km from town; town bus No 9 runs into town, or take a taxi (RM25). Regular connections with KL (MAS, AirAsia), Subang and Penang (Firefly).

Airline offices AirAsia office at the airport. MAS, ground floor, Komplek Yakin, Jln Gajah Mati (opposite the clock tower), T09-744 7000 and T09-744 0557 at the airport.

Bus

City buses and some long-distance express buses leave from the Central Bus Station, Jln Hilir Pasar. Many long-distance buses also depart from Jln Hamzah, 2 km from the city centre (RM8 taxi ride). (Check which terminal your bus leaves from.) Buses to Gua Musang and Pasir Puteh and Kuala Besut (for Perhentian Islands, RM6, 1½ hrs) also depart from here. Regular connections with Grik, Kuala Terengganu (RM14.20), Kuantan (RM31.40), KL (RM40.10), JB and Singapore (both RM77), Penang (RM37.40), Melaka (RM52.90), Mersing (RM48.10), Temerloh (RM41.40), and other destinations.

Note Long-distance bus tickets sell out quickly. Book as early as possible. There are a string of booking offices by the Central Bus Station.

Car hire

Avis, Hotel Perdana, Jln Sultan Mahmud, T09-748 4457; South China Sea, airport, T09-774 4288; from Perdana Hotel; Pacific, T09-744 7610.

Taxi

Taxi station next to Central Bus Station, Jln Hilir Pasar. Destinations: Kuala Besut (RM50), Kuala Terengganu, Kuantan, KL, JB, Butterworth, Grik. Also taxis to Rantau Panjang (for Sungai Golok, Thailand).

Train

Wakaf Bharu station is 6 km out of town, across the Kelantan River. Bus Nos 19 or 27 run into town. Several daily connections with Singapore and KL via Gua Musang, Kuala Lipis, and Jerantut. The railway is slow but the scenery makes the journey worthwhile. The daily train to KL leaves at 1904 to arrive around 0755. The daily services to Singapore leave at 0718 (arrives 2202) and 2030 (arrives 1100)

⊙ Directory

Taman Negara National Park
p81, map p81

Mutiara Taman Negara Resort has an expensive mini-market (trekking and camping goods); a clinic (daily 0800-1615, 24 hrs for emergencies); a post office, laundry and library.

Kampong Cherating p84

Banks Nearest bank is at Kemaman, 12 km north. **Internet** Cherating Travel Post (next to Mimis); Cherating Library and Cyber Café ('Capacity.com'), closed Wed.

Kuala Terengganu p85, map p85

Banks Jln Sultan Ismail.
Internet Golden Wood Internet Café, 59 Jln Tok Lam. **Medical services** Hospital, Jln Peranginan (off Jln Sultan Mahmud), T09-623 3333. **Post office** GPO, Jln Sultan Zainal Abidin. **Telephone** Telekom, Jln Sultan Ismail.

Perhentian Islands p87

Banks No banks or ATMs and few hotels accept credit cards. Nearest ATM is in Jerteh. Most guesthouses will change money. **Internet** Upmarket resorts have expensive internet access. Also try Panorama, Long Beach and Perhentian Pro-Diver, Coral Bay.

Kota Bharu *p88, map p88*
Banks Money changers in the main shopping area. **Embassies and consulates** Royal Thai Consulate, 4426 Jln Pengkalan Chepa, T09-744 5266, thaicg@tm.net.my, Mon-Thu and Sat 0900-1200, 1330-1530. **Immigration** 3rd floor, Federal Bldg, Jln Bayam, T09-748 2120. **Medical services** Hospital, Jln Hospital, T09-748 5533. **Post office** Jln Sultan Ibrahim.

Contents

Footnotes

Index

Titles available in the Footprint *Focus* range

Latin America	UK RRP	US RRP
Bahia & Salvador	£7.99	$11.95
Brazilian Amazon	£7.99	$11.95
Brazilian Pantanal	£6.99	$9.95
Buenos Aires & Pampas	£7.99	$11.95
Cartagena & Caribbean Coast	£7.99	$11.95
Costa Rica	£8.99	$12.95
Cuzco, La Paz & Lake Titicaca	£8.99	$12.95
El Salvador	£5.99	$8.95
Guadalajara & Pacific Coast	£6.99	$9.95
Guatemala	£8.99	$12.95
Guyana, Guyane & Suriname	£5.99	$8.95
Havana	£6.99	$9.95
Honduras	£7.99	$11.95
Nicaragua	£7.99	$11.95
Northeast Argentina & Uruguay	£8.99	$12.95
Paraguay	£5.99	$8.95
Quito & Galápagos Islands	£7.99	$11.95
Recife & Northeast Brazil	£7.99	$11.95
Rio de Janeiro	£8.99	$12.95
São Paulo	£5.99	$8.95
Uruguay	£6.99	$9.95
Venezuela	£8.99	$12.95
Yucatán Peninsula	£6.99	$9.95

Asia	UK RRP	US RRP
Angkor Wat	£5.99	$8.95
Bali & Lombok	£8.99	$12.95
Chennai & Tamil Nadu	£8.99	$12.95
Chiang Mai & Northern Thailand	£7.99	$11.95
Goa	£6.99	$9.95
Gulf of Thailand	£8.99	$12.95
Hanoi & Northern Vietnam	£8.99	$12.95
Ho Chi Minh City & Mekong Delta	£7.99	$11.95
Java	£7.99	$11.95
Kerala	£7.99	$11.95
Kolkata & West Bengal	£5.99	$8.95
Mumbai & Gujarat	£8.99	$12.95

Africa & Middle East	UK RRP	US RRP
Beirut	£6.99	$9.95
Cairo & Nile Delta	£8.99	$12.95
Damascus	£5.99	$8.95
Durban & KwaZulu Natal	£8.99	$12.95
Fès & Northern Morocco	£8.99	$12.95
Jerusalem	£8.99	$12.95
Johannesburg & Kruger National Park	£7.99	$11.95
Kenya's Beaches	£8.99	$12.95
Kilimanjaro & Northern Tanzania	£8.99	$12.95
Luxor to Aswan	£8.99	$12.95
Nairobi & Rift Valley	£7.99	$11.95
Red Sea & Sinai	£7.99	$11.95
Zanzibar & Pemba	£7.99	$11.95

Europe	UK RRP	US RRP
Bilbao & Basque Region	£6.99	$9.95
Brittany West Coast	£7.99	$11.95
Cádiz & Costa de la Luz	£6.99	$9.95
Granada & Sierra Nevada	£6.99	$9.95
Languedoc: Carcassonne to Montpellier	£7.99	$11.95
Málaga	£5.99	$8.95
Marseille & Western Provence	£7.99	$11.95
Orkney & Shetland Islands	£5.99	$8.95
Santander & Picos de Europa	£7.99	$11.95
Sardinia: Alghero & the North	£7.99	$11.95
Sardinia: Cagliari & the South	£7.99	$11.95
Seville	£5.99	$8.95
Sicily: Palermo & the Northwest	£7.99	$11.95
Sicily: Catania & the Southeast	£7.99	$11.95
Siena & Southern Tuscany	£7.99	$11.95
Sorrento, Capri & Amalfi Coast	£6.99	$9.95
Skye & Outer Hebrides	£6.99	$9.95
Verona & Lake Garda	£7.99	$11.95

North America	UK RRP	US RRP
Vancouver & Rockies	£8.99	$12.95

Australasia	UK RRP	US RRP
Brisbane & Queensland	£8.99	$12.95
Perth	£7.99	$11.95

For the latest books, e-books and a wealth of travel information, visit us at:
www.footprinttravelguides.com.

footprinttravelguides.com

Join us on facebook for the latest travel news, product releases, offers and amazing competitions:
www.facebook.com/footprintbooks